BOLD

BRIEF GLIMPSES OF A LIFE OF RISK

J.A. JERNAY

Copyright © 2025 by J.A. Jernay

All rights reserved.

No part of this book may be reproduced in any form or by any electronic or mechanical means, including information storage and retrieval systems, without written permission from the author, except for the use of brief quotations in a book review.

ISBN (electronic): 978-1-960936-60-8

ISBN (print): 978-1-960936-61-5

CONTENTS

Preface	v
1. Role Models	1
2. A Word About Confidence	6
3. Adventuring Through Books	9
4. The Old College Try	11
5. The Washington Post: Staying Quiet	20
6. The Washington Post: Speaking Up	27
7. The Washington Post: Book World	33
8. The Hard Times	44
9. The Not-So-Great American Road Trip	50
10. A Young Cub in Hollywood	54
11. Dating In LA: Hot People, Cold Connections	66
12. Mt. Whitney: The Longest Day	70
13. The Teflon Drinker	74
14. The Vows Were Lies	78
15. Fluent in Confusion	82
16. Starting Over In South America	87
17. A Second Chance in the Second City	93
18. The Oldest Guy on the Field	99
19. Yes Is My Default Setting	106
20. In the Land of Sand and Minarets	111
21. My Job Fit Into My Backpack	119
22. Love in the Time of Lockdowns	129
23. A Note About the Future	134
Plotworks Publishing	136
Catalina	138
Plotworks Publishing	141

September 10	144
Plotworks Publishing	146
About the Author	147

PREFACE

I'm too young to have written this book, but I did it anyways.

I'm in my late forties, and in a lot of ways my life has restarted. A new wife, a new state, a new home, new furniture, new income, a new small publishing company, new friends, pondering a possible new infant in the future.

To get to this point, I've taken a lot of risks.

Risk is a concept that many young people don't understand, because their environment has been built to allow them to construct their own curated lives. They know how to color inside the lines.

It shouldn't be this way.

I won't win any friends saying this. After all, living the straight and narrow isn't new. Middle-class and upper-middle-class families have always demanded caution and conformity. But over the last fifteen years, North American parents have taken this caution to new extremes.

Call it helicopter parenting. Call it the new common sense. Call it a safety-minded life. Call it whatever you'd like. What's undeniable is that because of the new coddling, middle-class young people display a near-total aversion to risk. In fact, they display a near-total aversion to doing anything at all.

Compared with previous generations, they're—

- Not studying
- Not participating in sports
- Not getting jobs
- Not getting driver's licenses
- Not meeting their friends
- Not meeting in groups
- Not smoking
- Not drinking
- Not using drugs
- Not having sex

McKinsey Consulting Group even wrote a report about how Gen Z is different from previous generations.

You can argue some of that is good news. You can argue that our current crop of youngsters has matured more quickly than ones in the past did. You can argue that they won't pursue the stupid behaviors that lead to injury and premature death the way previous stupider generations did. You can argue that their prefrontal cortices are better developed at an earlier age. You can argue that they're old souls with a high level of emotional self-awareness.

You'd be right about all this. Personally, I'm excited that Gen Z could end the generational cycle of trauma and abuse in their families. That's something the older generations could never do; they never had the vocabulary or awareness. This generation, on the other hand, never stops talking about their mental health.

That's the good news.

On the other hand, these risk-averse behaviors are stopping young people from attempting to reach goals, any goals at all. But it's the act of reaching goals, or at least attempting to reach them, that leads to happiness and self-empowerment.

So this is a real problem.

On their current trajectory, members of Gen Z are probably not going to become everything they could be. People tend to get more risk-averse as they age, and this cohort is already acting like sixty-year-old people, battered by life, by the time they've graduated from high school.

I'd compare them to the Silent Generation: that quiet cohort born between 1928 and 1945. Too young to fight in World War II, that generation was born into the hunger and poverty of the Great Depression. As a result, the Silent Generation were some of the most risk-averse people ever created in modern America. They lived lives of radical caution, professionally and personally, afraid of putting a single toe out of line. They worked all their lives for the same corporation. They paid cash for their houses and then lived in them for forty or fifty years. Early on, they were even derisively called "radio babies", criticized by older generations for having grown up immersed in a new technology. (That last bit should sound familiar to our new digital natives.)

But humans need to take risks.

There is no doubt about this. Taking risks is how we grow, how we change, how we learn, and how we ultimately feel satisfied with our lives.

That's why I wrote this short book.

This little memoir in your hands illustrates the risks that I've taken in my life. It tries to show that risks come in many different flavors—from professional risks to romantic ones, from geographic to intellectual, from financial to athletic. Some have paid off very well for me. Many others turned out to be a wash, and didn't move the needle one way or the other. A few were total failures.

But you won't lead a full life unless you take some of them.

As Ray Bradbury wrote, jump off that cliff, and build your wings on the way down. Here are some stories of my leap.

1
ROLE MODELS

MY FATHER

I was lucky that I had a few risk-takers to model myself after.

Before I was born, my dad ditched a job in a law firm after a single year. At the ripe age of twenty-six, he saw a future for himself as a solo practitioner. He wanted a career as a criminal defense attorney in private practice—with his own office, secretary, telephone, and wall of books. To be his own boss.

To get his name known in our community, he decided to run for local judge. Again, he was twenty-six years old, so this was a ludicrous decision. He knew he wouldn't win, but he persuaded my mother to walk with him for nearly six months, knocking on literally every door in the city. She was pregnant with me at the time. He lost the race, but not as badly as he'd thought, and his legal practice was soon growing.

The risk paid off.

He has a great radio voice, and later he hosted a biweekly "Ask the Lawyer" hour on a local Detroit radio program. I think it was on WXYZ. I remember sitting in the lobby of the radio station, watching him host it.

More importantly to my own life, my dad wrote several legal books, technical guides to legal defense. One of them eventually became the bible of his profession in the state of Michigan. It's still in use today, over forty years later, and my friends who've entered the legal field have told me they consult it.

All I knew, as a child, was that he kept a copy of a book in the backseat of his Buick. So I just assumed that this was normal—my dad wrote a book, which meant that all men wrote books. Right? You can draw a direct line from that book in the backseat of the car to my own choices as a writer and publisher.

MY MOTHER

She's a force of nature, and that's understating it. My mother has taken risks with her life nearly every chance she could, and she resents anybody who prevents her from taking more.

She's been a teacher and a counselor in violent inner-city high schools. She's been thrown up against the blackboard by armed Black Panther-style revolutionaries, a weapon held against her head. In a different role, years later, she sued her union for failing to support her in a dispute with her employer—and won. In her fifties, she completed a three-day Marine Corps training at Parris Island, South Carolina. In her sixties, she became a Red Cross responder for national disaster zones. Over a span of about nine years, she was deployed to 17 different natural disasters to provide mental health counseling for those affected. Hurricane Sandy in New York, wildfires in California, flooding in North Dakota—she did them all. As a local Red Cross volunteer, she provided the same mental health counseling to people who'd just lost their homes due to fires, usually in the middle of the night in the worst neighborhoods of Detroit. On top of it all, she walked across northern Spain on the Camino de Santiago.

The only thing that finally slowed her risk-taking? Old age.

MY COUSIN

Max is ten years older than me, and I grew up listening to him play and perform the piano. He was hugely talented, with fingers of an angel that ran lightly over the arpeggios. He attended Oberlin Conservatory of Music and the University of Michigan before launching a big regional career as a pianist. He recorded and sold several albums, played in lobbies of expensive hotels, kept a studio of hundreds of students, and played for more than a few celebrity weddings.

I can't say I idolized him. In fact, I went out of my way to avoid playing the piano, because it's cold in the shadows. I switched instead to guitar. Still, as a teenager, I learned from Max that a career in the arts was possible, and that you needed confidence, talent, and business acumen to make it happen.

I also learned from him that boldness with women paid off. I watched him flirt with anything wearing a smile and a bra. He loved to use me as a prop. Teenage me was happy to play Robin to his Batman. All of it showed me how women responded to an assertive man. I made mental notes.

Over the decades, his life took some unexpected turns due to a series of bad decisions. Let's just say he's got some inner demons. Today, he's changed his last name and now lives a quiet life in Europe.

But I was his young sidekick, quietly watching his boldness, and taking notes.

MY SISTER

My younger sister, Allison, absorbed many of the same lessons about risk that I did. She flew off to London immediately after college graduation, married her English boyfriend, and stayed for six years, earning EU citizenship. That takes some sauce.

After the marriage ended, she flew to New Jersey to meet a strange guy she'd met on Facebook. They had a thousand things in common, most especially surfing. It was a risky move for safety reasons, and she didn't tell anybody in the family what she was doing. Fortunately, it worked out: they've been together fifteen years as of this writing, and Jim is a part of the family. He's also probably the most intense guy I know. He does everything at top speed, with maximum emotion and commitment, from morning to night, every day. Jim needs to write his own memoir of boldness.

In 2020, my sister took another risk: she left the company where she'd been employed for nine years in order to open her own interior design firm. She nervously took out a lease on office space and began directly competing with her former boss, serving the southern Jersey shore. Right now, she's got two employees and a year's worth of work booked ahead. I knew she'd be successful, and I'm proud. In fact, everybody was sure of her success except for her, which goes to show that we are not the best judge of our own talents.

2
A WORD ABOUT CONFIDENCE

Being assertive isn't the same as being aggressive. Assertive people are unconcerned with retribution. Assertive people fit within civilized society. When I was growing up, my mother demanded that I be assertive, but she punished me if I got aggressive.

The one quality that an assertive person exhibits is confidence. Let me define the term, as I see it.

Confidence is not the belief that you will always win. Instead, *confidence is the knowledge that you will survive every outcome.*

It's not loud either. Real confidence is quiet, burbling along under a person's surface. It doesn't need to announce itself.

There isn't one way to build confidence either. I see three ways.

1. ***Natural***. There are some lucky individuals who slide into this world with an innate sense of their own strength. It's probably due to a gene

receptor that scientists will discover a few decades from now.
2. ***Cultural***. It's defined by the tiny but important boosts that you receive, or don't receive, in your daily life. It's based on your height, weight, race, gender, religion, language, and income. In the Western world, this takes the shape of white male privilege, which is often invisible if you're a white male who was raised around other white males. It's like asking a fish to identify what water is. But step outside of that bubble, as I have, and you'll see it more clearly.
3. ***Earned***. You can set goals for yourself and try to achieve them. It doesn't matter whether you succeed, fail, or land somewhere in the middle. You'll earn confidence either way. To my eyes, this is what young people lack today, compared with previous generations. This is also what Will Ferrell built his entire acting career on—characters who display a ridiculous amount of unearned confidence.

Once you build a habit of assertiveness, life seems full of possibilities. You can gain access to the Kennedy Center in Washington, D.C., even when it's closed, by knocking on the glass door and persuading a cleaning guy to let you in (me, age 18). You can tell President Bill Clinton, while shaking his hand in the White House, that you're planning to follow in his footsteps (me, age 19). You can relocate to a new city on the other side of the United States, and build a new life, knowing that you'll survive and maybe thrive (me, four times).

By the way, I didn't want to become president. I just wanted to flatter the most powerful person on earth.

No matter what, assertive people know that they are the final arbiter of their own lives. They don't wait for permission. They tell themselves and the world what they're going to do, and they try to do it.

3
ADVENTURING THROUGH BOOKS

You can be bold inside your own head.

I was a bookworm, and Tuesday night visits to the public library were a highlight of the week. At home, I typically cycled through four to five books at a time. In the tiny extra bedroom that we used as a study, my reading chair was a squeaky black vinyl number with padded armrests. I used that thing for almost fifteen years, until I lent it to a guy in college named Alex who then avoided me for the next two years and never gave it back.

Lesson learned.

But I read everything I could find. My favorites were mysteries and thrillers. In sixth grade I discovered Agatha Christie and read at least forty whodunits in a single year. I devoured all the James Bond titles (hilariously bad) and all the Sherlock Holmes short stories (stupendously good). Later, I tore through the Tom Clancy titles, especially *The Hunt For Red October*, though I didn't like the old-grouchy-white-guy resentment that bubbled up in later stories like *The Sum of All Fears*. Over in speculative fiction, I soaked up Philip Jose Farmer, Roger Zelazny, Arthur C. Clarke,

Margaret Weis & Tracy Hickman's *Darksword* trilogy. I read middle-grade encyclopedias and especially loved books of trivia. I still love those.

And I talked. I yammered on endlessly, about all the stories I was reading, all the trivia I was learning, and anything else that crossed my mind. Out of my mouth came constant stream of chatter, jokes, facts, made-up stories. I asked myself questions, then answered them. On long car rides, my parents even paid me a penny a minute to shut up. I usually made a nickel.

I didn't feel any fear. I saw the world as a place to be explored and understood.

All of this inquiry, in turn, led to higher grades, as I was comfortable with analyzing words and asking questions. That, in turn, led to high performance in high school, with AP classes and public speaking competitions. And that, in turn led to a full-tuition scholarship to a good university.

Seizing books, extracting ideas, diving into stories. Turning the world around in my hands, questioning it, discussing it. This was a habit of intellectual and creative boldness. We can all do it. Most of us just don't care enough to do so.

4
THE OLD COLLEGE TRY

I don't like to admit this, but I had to be convinced by my family to study at Oxford University.

My home university offered a lot of study abroad options. One of them, open only to students in the honors program, featured a special arrangement with Keble College, Oxford University. It sent three students per year to study there, all of whom had to be vetted by the venerable Oxford dons.

For some reason, I didn't think to apply. This book is about boldness, and taking chances, but I somehow fell flat on that one. Maybe I should chalk it up to the distractions of sophomore year. Anyhow, my parents back home somehow learned about the program and urged me to do it.

You can read about my experiences in *The Oxford Diaries*, a journal I kept of my time at the third-oldest university in the world. I didn't know what I was going to do with the diaries, but I put a lot of work into them, handwriting the entries in a red leatherbound journal. The decision to write something that nobody asked for has paid off decades later—*The Oxford Diaries* has hundreds of sales and library borrows, in both print and electronic, even though it currently has zero reviews and I've never bothered to advertise it.

Also, I found that having Oxford University on one's resume is a small superpower. Though the effect has worn off a bit as the decades have passed, those two words sometimes still impress employers and clients. In my mid-forties, while on a business trip to the Arabic world, I stood up in a crowded auditorium of five hundred people as a speaker read off my accomplishments. When he said the words *Oxford University*, I heard the crowd audibly ooh.

The lesson: Cachet is real. If you can find a way to get a little, I recommend it.

THE SAME YEAR I went to Oxford, I decided to spend part of Christmas break traveling through Europe. I settled on Rome, Vienna, and Prague. I didn't speak Italian, German, or Czech. I'd never even been to Europe. I didn't know the currencies. I didn't even plan anything, not even hotels.

I just went. I built my wings on the way down.

What was supposed to be a straight shot from London to Paris to Rome was interrupted by a French railroad strike. I ended up traveling for 48 straight hours across nine different connecting trains, all improvised by close study of the railway timetables. For a skinny twenty-year-old kid who was wet behind the ears and had never traveled internationally before, this could've been a big setback. But I did it.

I had friends in Rome, but in Prague I knew nobody. To communicate, I was reduced to grunting and pointing. The city had been under the Soviet rule just a few years earlier, and I overestimated their willingness to help young Western travelers. It was freezing cold, and I felt like a failure. I felt like I'd overshot my limits.

THE NEXT MONTH, back at my home university in the U.S., I sat in the assistant dean's office and announced my decision.

"I want to pursue a master's degree concurrently with my bachelor's degree," I said.

"In what program?" she asked.

"Rhetoric," I answered.

I had enough credits to graduate after three years, but my full-tuition scholarship covered four years of education. It would've been foolish to waste that money. So I grew intent on forcing my way into a master's degree. I'd been planning it for months, like a tactical strike.

"You'll have to submit a GRE score," the assistant dean said.

I slid my results across the table to her. Knowing the question was coming, I'd taken the exam a few weeks earlier.

"Oh, thank you," she said. Her eyes scanned the numbers. "Well done. This score will do. Anyways, you'll have to talk to Dr. Moss and get her permission, since it's her program. Have you contacted her?"

"She wants me in the program," I said. "We've been emailing each other for months. I took a course from her a year ago, so she knows what I can do."

"Well," the assistant dean said, "I suppose that's settled. I'll get in touch with her."

Our exchange continued as I watched her grope around

for more objections. There were a few more details she wanted answered.

"I guess it's all done then," she finally said.

We shook hands and I thanked her and stood up. I left the office and strutted down the hall.

Years later, I realized the importance of what I'd just done. With some careful preparation, I'd asserted myself into saving nearly fifty thousand dollars on my own education.

That was over a quarter of a century ago. When I talk with clients today about my educational background, I often lead with my master's degree. I thank my younger self for being so bold.

Going to meet Chinese action movie star Jackie Chan in New York City was a terrible risk that backfired on me spectacularly. Later, however, it paid off.

I had been the features editor of my university newspaper. Every week, I brainstormed writing assignments and handed them out to staff, sometimes scribbling them myself when a writer stopped returning my messages. Working under deadline brought out my best self, and I was sure that journalism was in my future.

It wasn't, but that's a different story.

As features editor, I received all kinds of free swag and tickets and offers in the mail. I opened free compact discs from record labels, introducing me to artists I'd never heard of, like Chucklehead and Patty Larkin. I got free tickets to advance movie screenings every Tuesday night, which I used to impress girls and entertain friends. I even called up ticket offices across Washington, D.C., introduced myself as the features editor, and straight-up asked for free tickets to live performances. They sometimes said yes. I attended shows at Ford's Theater, the Kennedy Center, and other places, all for free. I was a poor student, but I was living the high life.

Then I got a unique letter: Sony Pictures offered me an all-expense paid trip to New York City to see an advance screening of a Jackie Chan movie. He would be there to take questions. All I needed to do was write a review.

I replied yes, and Sony sent me reimbursement for the train ticket and the hotel. It was a deadly cold February weekend, and stepping off the Amtrak at Penn Station I began to think I'd made a mistake. I don't remember anything about the movie, not even the name, but I do remember meeting Jackie Chan afterwards. He was a manic ball of energy who spoke almost no English.

After the screening, I spent a miserable, freezing night in a shared room in a midtown hostel. I left at five am.

Back in Washington, D.C., I wrote my review. On Wednesday night, I handed it to our newspaper's advisor, Tim Lowe, expecting the usual stamp of approval.

Tim Lowe was a portly man with a droopy moustache and a scoundrel's glint in his eyes. As a younger man, he'd been a hotshot economics reporter at *The Washington Post*, assigned to Latin America. In fact, he'd been such a success that the bosses recalled him to the newsroom and made him a national desk editor, where he was still working at that time. He and I had always gotten along well. I loved his raconteur's tales, and he loved an audience. He also thought highly of my writing.

"I need to talk to you," he said to me.

I followed him into a small private room down the hall from the main newspaper office. It was lit with a single small green banker's lamp. I sat on a chair, and to my surprise he stood over me.

"You went to New York to review a movie?" he said. His voice was serious.

I gulped. "Yeah, I did."

"That's a long way to go to see a movie."

"Well, I got to meet Jackie Chan. He's the biggest movie star in Asia."

He ignored that. "Did Sony Pictures pay for your trip?"

"Yeah."

"How much did they give you?"

I told him the amount. "It was for train and hotel."

He rubbed his face in frustration. "You shouldn't have done that."

"Why not?"

He pulled up a chair and sat down. Now we were level. He began to teach me about professional ethics. "That is called pay-for-play journalism," he explained. "We have to remain impartial in everything. If you accept their money for a review, you can't be impartial."

Just like that, the clouds parted. I understood what I'd done wrong, ethically. It was a small mistake, but I also saw for the first time how people could be easily corrupted. It'd just happened to me, on a small scale, without my realizing.

"I'm sorry," I said.

"You're forgiven." He smiled.

"So now what?"

"You have to send that money back, if you want to publish the review."

I sighed. My bank account was limited. But I went ahead and returned the money to Sony. I never published the review.

To my surprise, Tim Lowe and I drew a little closer together after that. The following autumn he made an introduction for me that was hugely pivotal to the next decade of my life.

He recommended me for a job at *The Washington Post*. It was his employer, so he was putting his reputation on the line.

You would think that I could remember exactly how it happened—whether it was my idea or his—but I don't. Today, all I know is that I found myself in the human resources department of the fabled fifth-floor newsroom, wearing a collar shirt with a tie, making my case to a friendly human resources woman about how much I didn't want to be a political reporter.

"Excuse me?" she said.

"I *don't* want to be a political reporter," I said. "Everybody who comes into this newsroom probably hopes to be assigned the White House beat. Everybody here thinks they'll become the next Bob Woodward and take down a president. I don't want that. I want to become a writer and a publisher of books. And having a job here would be ideal because I'll be surrounded by people who are writing at a high professional level every day. I think it'll benefit me to pick up their habits."

I really said that, in roughly those words. I wanted to differentiate myself from the hordes of smart, young, cocky white guys whose resumés were undoubtedly stacked inside her desk. I was smart, young, cocky white guy too—but a different type of one.

"That's interesting," she said. "Who is your role model?"

"Tom Wolfe," I said. "He worked here in the nineteen sixties for a couple years. Then he moved on." I lifted my palms to the sky. "So that's me."

I got the job. They hired me as a part-time night news aide, the absolute bottom of the food chain. Twenty years old, making the princely amount of twelve dollars an hour. I felt like a rich man.

Was that bold? Getting the interview wasn't. Tim Lowe's referral was an old-fashioned connection. But my interview was inspired. I didn't go in with my hat in hand, begging and nervous and agreeable. Instead, I showed the company how our two circles overlapped: my goals and their needs. I've used that assertive interview style ever since.

A FEW MONTHS EARLIER, I had been homeless for three weeks.

My dormitory kicked me out on June 7, but my new off-campus house wasn't ready until July 1. Most of my friends had gone home that month. My back against the wall, I took my only remaining option.

I slept in the student newspaper office.

I'd volunteered to look after the office during the summer, since I was staying in town doing an internship at *The Washington Monthly* magazine. So I had ownership of the keys. Without telling anybody, I carried all my belongings up four flights of stairs and stored them in the office. I put my sheets on the beat-up plaid couch where we had editorial meetings. I ate noodles out of a small electric cooker I plugged into the power strip under a desk. I rode my bike to work in the day, then showered at the university gym later in the afternoon. I sneaked into dormitories to do laundry.

The office was located in a student services building on campus, and the security set a door alarm each night, so I made sure to arrive back before 10 pm. I also discovered that a night security guard made his rounds each night at 11 pm. Each night, I listened for his footsteps and turned off my lamp, in case he saw the light under the doorway.

This didn't seem like a big risk at the time—it still doesn't today—but people have told me that this was outrageous. Maybe I could've gotten booted out of the school, but that wasn't likely. I just did what I had to do to survive for a few weeks.

5
THE WASHINGTON POST: STAYING QUIET

At The Washington Post, I spent fifteen months working on the Metro, news, and foreign desks. I was a full- or part-time student by day, and a copy boy at a world-famous newspaper at night. It was an education in and of itself, and to this day it remains my favorite place I've ever worked.

I started out on the local desk, answering phones, running copy, doing whatever the editors asked of me. We were prohibited from ever hanging up on the public, no matter what. We used to get a paranoid schizophrenic from Iowa who would call up to tell us about how the CIA was spreading pieces of broken glass on the roads to puncture his tires. He'd talk for hours. After a while, I just set the phone on the desk and let him ramble.

Later, I transferred to the news desk. It was kind of a promotion, because the news desk was the center of the newsroom, the very beating heart of Washington political journalism. We called it The Hub.

This area was a pressure-filled environment. My desk was situated directly in front of the glass wall of the office of the then-managing editor, Bob Kaiser. Nervous, I felt like he was watching my back, and I stayed on my best behavior. He definitely wasn't.

The Hub sat next to me: an island of eight different connected workspaces. It was here where the top editors laid out the front page every night. I remember more than one agitated staff writer coming up to the news desk to complain about the placement of his piece, or to make a last-minute pitch for his article to be included on the front page. I watched as the editors professionally reassured these writers before dismissing them. The newshole (the daily space available for stories) was large at the Post, but in an organization of 700 reporters and editors, not everybody's contributions made the cut. In fact, the ratio was 1 to 2—for every one article that was published, two more were trashed. It was brutal.

If you want to see what the newsroom looked like, just watch the Academy Award-winning film *All the President's Men* (1976), which is the story of how the editors and reporters at the Post drove the investigation of the Watergate scandal in the early 1970s. The filmmakers reproduced the newsroom exactly as it appeared, even taking real Washington Post trash to put in the fake newsroom's trash cans. The newsroom hadn't changed at all by the time I was there a quarter of a century later. You can see my desk in several scenes.

My job at the news desk primarily revolved around the front section and the front page. I ran proofs downstairs to layout, coordinated stuff with the printers, distributed copies of the front page to the entire newsroom, answered phones, connected people to editors, and even faxed the front page to our archenemy, the *New York Times*. They did the same to us out of professional courtesy, and the top editors always pounced on these transmissions. One night, an hour before the usual exchange, the Times accidentally sent me a mockup of their future front page. I was greeted like a hero by the news desk, and even by the managing editor. I had obtained secret intel on the enemy.

For a while, the hardest part of the job was learning to ignore the fact that I was working alongside Bob Woodward. His office was about thirty feet to my right, and Woodward was always passing behind my back, chatting with other staffers. He typically helmed the paper every other weekend, when the executive editor and managing editor were off. Sometimes, at seven o'clock on a Sunday evening, it was just me, Woodward, and five or six other people in the entire newsroom. It took me a long time to get used to the fact that the man who broke open the Watergate scandal and destroyed the entire presidency of Richard Nixon was regularly bringing sandwiches and ice cream for me and the other members of the Sunday skeleton crew.

We chatted a little here and there, but mostly I just eavesdropped on him, like any curious young writer would. I can report that Woodward is a terrific listener. He has a very agreeable, friendly personality, which I attribute to his Midwestern upbringing. Whenever he called the Hub from home, I noticed his phone manner: he's strong but smooth in your ear. And he has a dogged manner of asking the same question five or ten or thirty different times until he gets the answer that he needs.

I didn't want to be him, but being *near* him was inspiring.

If you know anything about the Post, there's another name inextricably linked with it: the late Benjamin Bradlee. He was the famous executive editor who stood by and supported Woodward and Bernstein during their Watergate investigation, and who made the decision to publish portions of the Pentagon Papers. He'd stepped down years before and was now a vice president at-large, free to bask in the admiration of everyone within eyesight. On the rare occasion when Bradlee entered the newsroom, it was like the pope had arrived. Writers and editors dropped everything and ran over to worship at his feet.

I often saw him eating dinner in the Post cafeteria, surrounded by fawning admirers who hung on his every word. I used to sit nearby, trying to eavesdrop. Evidently he noticed, because he glared at me once, so I stopped doing that. That's what happens when you try to get too close to privilege.

Those two weren't the only luminaries in the newsroom at the time. The very elderly Herblock was still working in the late nineties. In case you don't know the name—he died shortly thereafter, in 2001—Herbert Block had been America's most famous political cartoonist for about half a century. Let me put it this way: Herblock was so old that he had won his first Pulitzer Prize *before my parents had even been born.*

Every night I watched the eighty-something legend hobble through the newsroom, clutching the whiteboard with that day's drawing. He always headed towards an editor named Peter, seeking his approval for that day's drawing, even though Peter was forty years younger than him. It felt like watching a prehistoric fossil in motion. I was in awe.

AT THE POST, I suffered one embarrassing interaction that stuck with me.

My first task at four o'clock every afternoon was to hand

out photocopies of a preliminary front-page mockup to every editor in the newsroom. Why they didn't do this over our software system, I don't know. Maybe old habits refused to die. Maybe they liked to feel the paper in their hands.

The problem was that I couldn't always distinguish between editors and writers. People didn't wear signs announcing their roles, and editors sat in a variety of workspaces. So I was forced to ask people, again and again, "Excuse me, are you an editor?"

Hundreds of people worked in the newsroom. It took me a long time to learn people's faces.

In my second week, I noticed a man I hadn't seen before sitting at a chair at an empty workspace. He was black.

"Excuse me, sir, are you an editor?" I asked.

The man shot me a very irritated look. "Yes, I'm the assistant foreign editor."

He said it in a way that meant *you'd better not forget it*.

"Sorry," I said. I handed him the photocopy and moved along.

I saw him again later that week, and his manner had changed. He literally bowed at me. "And how are you today, sir?" he said, in an exaggerated theatrical accent.

I was taken aback. We were strangers. "Fine? How about you?"

"Glad to hear it!"

He delivered me a big cheese-eating smile. I didn't know this man at all, but he went on like that whenever we'd run into each other. I'd see him at the elevator, and he'd smile exaggeratedly and make a grand gesture to join him inside. It felt so fake. It was confusing too, until it finally hit me.

This guy was pulling an Uncle Tom.

He'd misinterpreted my dumb question on our first

encounter as a coded racist comment. He most likely assumed that I was a privileged white kid, maybe one with an important racist daddy, He was probably guessing that I didn't believe that a black man could ever be an editor. (None of that was true, except for the fact that I'm white.)

I also got the sense that he was covering his bases, just in case I might be worth knowing later.

In short, his behavior was embarrassing. This man was a quarter of a century older than me. He was highly accomplished. In retrospect, I think his sudden bootlicking was a Southern thing—he'd grown up in rural South Carolina. I'm not going to reveal this man's name, but he's well known. In fact, if you've ever watched presidential election coverage on CNN, MSNBC, or Meet the Press, you've almost certainly seen and listened to him.

But I'm not from the South. I'm from Detroit, where black people absolutely don't lick anybody's boots. In fact, we Detroiters of all colors pride ourselves on our pride, and we know how to defend ourselves—maybe a bit too much. Let's just say it's a well-known characteristic of my city.

I understand now, years later, that racism was present in that newsroom. Even though my direct boss and the human resources director who hired me were both black women, there were very few other people of color there. Only one other news aide was a black woman, and she was strangely irritable with me, even yelling at me for an imaginary offense that she'd cooked up in her head. Today, I see that she must've been feeling out of place, and I was a convenient whipping boy because we were at the same level.

It seems like not much has changed in the intervening decades, unfortunately. In 2022, the Washington Post Guild issued a long statement about racism in their newsroom, which you can read about here.

OVERALL, I stayed quiet in the newsroom.

I worked second shift, so the newsroom was bustling when I arrived in the late afternoon. It gradually quieted down as reporters and editors trickled out and we put the paper to bed at nine-fifteen, when the first of five different editions was due to the printers on the ground floor. Small tweaks were made at that point, but our job was mostly done, and sometimes I was out the door by ten pm. On busy news nights I stayed until midnight.

As a lowly assistant, I wasn't expected to act boldly. But I did find three opportunities to make myself known.

6
THE WASHINGTON POST: SPEAKING UP

Once, on Halloween night, the chief Metro desk editor was editing a story about a man dressed like a marshmallow who'd accidentally set himself on fire at a party. It was eight-thirty, and I overheard him asking if anybody knew how to spell the name of a famous brand of marshmallow.

"Did you say Stay Puft?" I said.

The editor looked irritated that I was speaking with him. My job was not to suggest anything editorial. But my mouth sometimes has a mind of its own.

"Yesss," he replied cautiously.

"Puft is four letters, spelled with a t."

"Are you sure?" he asked, swiveling to face me. The man was in his forties. I was barely twenty-one.

"I'm getting a master's degree in English," I replied confidently.

There was a tense moment while he decided whether to trust me about the spelling of the name of a fictional marshmallow.

"But you're *sure*?" he said again.

I grew exasperated. "I've seen *Ghostbusters* at least fifteen times."

"Why does that matter?"

I realized that he hadn't seen that movie, or maybe had forgotten. "The monster terrorizing New York City at the end of the movie is a giant Stay Puft marshmallow man."

"Oh." That seemed to persuade him. He entered the spelling, and I walked off. The earth continued spinning on its axis.

―――

My second move at the newspaper occurred on the last Sunday in August.

By this point, I'd been at the paper for almost a year, and I'd been asked to work as a weekend aide on the foreign desk. This meant that I called foreign correspondents all over the world to bother them about deadlines, to find out when they were going to file their stories. Some editors like to ask those questions themselves, so I just patched them over. Honestly, there really wasn't much to do. Unlike the news desk, the foreign desk gave me time to do my classwork during the shift.

At about nine o'clock that Sunday night, the football-field-sized newsroom was silent. There were literally only three people remaining. Carl, the weekend night editor, was a rambunctious alcoholic from North Carolina who loved the expression *shitfire*. He said it the way other people said *okay*. The second person, Kenny, was the night foreign desk editor; he was mild-mannered and had worked for years at *Stars and Stripes*, the daily American military newspaper read primarily by people overseas.

The third person was me.

I'd just returned from running through the building on my usual route. I'd nodded to all the deaf people working in the third-floor layout area. Post publisher Katharine Graham had hired over a hundred deaf people to put out the paper every night. We communicated mostly through written notes. I'd moved quickly on my usual path through the ground floor printing presses, nodding at the guys in their ink-smudged overalls. We waved at each other a lot, but rarely spoke. The roar of the machines, the lines of newspapers spindling past everywhere, made it impossible to hear, even for the few who weren't deaf.

I'd just sat down in my office chair on the fifth floor again when the foreign desk phone rang.

"I'll get it," said Kenny.

I shrugged. If he wanted to do my job, that was fine. He picked up the phone and listened.

"She *what?*" he suddenly shouted, phone to ear.

I looked over, alarmed. Kenny had literally climbed on top of his chair. He was standing there, his mouth open, phone to ear.

I turned to look at Carl, a short distance away. "What going on?" I said.

"Shitfire, boy, I don't know," he said, straightening up, "but this is gonna be something."

Kenny hung up the phone and turned to both of us. "Princess Diana has been killed," he said.

Neither of them wasted any time. Carl told me to start calling editors at home to come into the newsroom, immediately. I got in touch with three of them; one was already watching the television coverage.

"Listen up," said Kenny to me, his voice tight with urgency. "In a few seconds, you're going to get a call from

Samuel in London. He's going to dictate a piece. You take the dictation and send it straight over to me."

Samuel was the Post foreign correspondent in London. He was one of the few foreign correspondents who I hadn't spoken with.

Quickly I opened a new document on my screen. As I did that, my phone rang.

"Hello," I said.

A man's deep, imperious voice filled my ear. "Begin dictation. On Sunday night, an entire nation was plunged into mourning by the tragic death in an automobile accident of the people's princess, Diana of Wales. At approximately…"

Cradling the phone in my ear, I listened to his voice as my fingers struggled to keep up on the keyboard. I was and still am a fast typist—I can usually hit 70 or 80 words per minute—but this was impossible at that moment. In the late nineties, the Post was still using an awful proprietary software system called RoadRunner. It's long dead now, and at that moment I was wishing for a swift murder. It was lagging badly, and the keys on my computer weren't even pressing down correctly. Plus I was nervous.

After two or three minutes, I had fallen behind Samuel's words. He kept droning on, trying to sound authoritative, but I could also hear the guy improvising the story too. He used no facts, no numbers, no locations, no cause of death, no quotes, no authorities, no details whatsoever. Diana's death was too new for any of that. He was simply making up vague sentences so we could cram it into the paper for the third edition.

In short, he was bullshitting.

But I was too scared to tell him that I'd lost the thread. So, taking a deep breath, I began to ignore him completely.

Instead, I started typing my own analysis of the death of Princess Diana, which I knew nothing about. I struck a tone of ceremonial sadness and stayed appropriately vague.

In truth, my version wasn't going to be any better or any worse than his. We were equally good with words, and neither one of us knew anything concrete.

At last, Samuel ended the dictation. I hung up the phone. Kenny immediately barked, "Where is it?"

"I have to fix the typos," I said.

"No time!" he said. "Send it right now. It costs five thousand dollars for every ten minutes we hold the presses."

Kenny had literally stopped the presses. And he hadn't done it in the clichéd way you see in television or movies, screaming like a crazy person. He'd just picked up the phone and said it quietly, like a normal person.

The typos had to stay. I immediately sent Kenny the piece. He immediately forwarded it to layout, who immediately poured it onto the front page under a banner headline. Then the powerful presses under the building immediately started printing it, hundreds of thousands of copies.

The next day, *The Washington Post*'s main coverage of the death of Princess Diana was half written by yours truly, under Samuel's name. A college student barely old enough to drink, wearing jeans and sneakers, improvising the way he thought the nation's most important political newspaper ought to memorialize the dead princess of the most important monarchy in the world. Furthermore, with the newspaper's daily circulation of 800,000 at that point, I'd personally committed millions of typos in print.

Nobody ever said anything to me about the piece. Kenny never brought it up. Samuel in London never said anything either. He was too busy doing actual reporting in the following days and weeks. I'm not sure how I benefitted from that moment of high-pressure journalism. The best thing I can say is that I got away with it without getting fired.

Still, I'd been quietly champing at the bit to get my own name in the paper, and it would happen a couple months later.

7
THE WASHINGTON POST: BOOK WORLD

During my last six months at the newspaper, I applied to work in the Book World section, located on the fourth floor, next to the Home & Garden editorial section. This was the literary wing of the Post empire. It was an excellent chance to see the world of publishing from a different perspective, one more in line with my ambitions.

I leapt on the opportunity, even though a couple of other assistants at my level accused me of "cutting in line" by applying after only a year at the paper. I didn't understand that complaint then, and I don't understand it now. There was no line. Today, I would've caught the distinct scent of jealousy.

None of the people working in the books section were type-A personalities, which was a relief from the hectic pressure upstairs in the newsroom. The editor, Nina King (now sadly passed away), welcomed me and showed me my simple responsibilities. Three days a week, I was to wheel a huge cart of packages from the mailroom up to the book section storage room. There, I would open the books for the next several hours, look through them, weed them out as I saw fit, and arrange a lineup of new titles for the editors to consider reviewing.

For a grown-up bookworm like me, it was Christmas morning, every morning. I loved going to work. My hands ached from all the tearing of cardboard, but I didn't care. I was being paid to explore new ideas, and I didn't have to sit behind a desk while doing it: this was a mildly physical job, which suited me just fine.

We typically received eighty books per day, but the newspaper only reviewed one, sometimes two. At least half of the submissions were obviously low quality. They had poor cover designs, or ugly interiors, or awkward organization, or bizarrely obscure topics, or a lack of focus. The discarded titles I sometimes placed in a box in the hallway on a cart for other employees to take. Every day I found a few titles that interested me, and I carried those home in by backpack. During those six months, I grabbed about two hundred books for myself. I still have a beautifully illustrated version of *The Hobbit*.

My coworkers were erudite bookworms, of course. I came to know Michael Dirda pretty well; he still reviews for the Post, even in his late seventies. Another famous critic, Jonathan Yardley, popped in once a week to paw through the new titles.

"Hey Jonathan," I said one day.

"What," he replied. He was hiding in the shelving, perusing the many titles that I'd stored there. He had a reputation for being cranky, but he was always decent with me. I felt bad for him because he'd once published a four-hundred-page family history that, in his words, had sold almost zero copies. He sometimes liked to invite the Book World staff to his house in Baltimore for homemade jambalaya.

"Working here," I said, "has shown me just how many bad books are in the world."

"Oh goodness yes," he replied. "There are far more bad ones than good ones."

Yardley didn't know, but that simple sentence changed my life. It made me resolve to improve myself to become one of the good ones.

ONE DAY I ripped open a package to find a hardcover copy of *The Long Hard Road Out of Hell*, a brand-new memoir written by Marilyn Manson. He had been terrorizing the music charts for a few years, sowing panic in straightlaced Christian communities across the country. Manson came from a long tradition of boogeymen, and he was controversial.

I featured it prominently on my book display. Michael Dirda came in and passed straight over it.

"Don't you think we should review that Manson book?" I said. "Everybody's been talking about him. And it's high quality."

"Mm," he said. That meant nothing. He may not have even known who Manson was. Michael's heart has always been with light British fiction from the early twentieth century.

I tried the same pitch with Jabari Asim, another editor who later became the head of *The Crisis* magazine at the NAACP. As a black man, he wasn't too enthralled with the idea of reviewing Manson either.

But I wouldn't be deterred. I knew I was a good writer, and this book could be my sneaky way to a Post byline. I was twenty-one years old, enrolled at a very religious university. I didn't like Manson at all, but I felt I understood this weirdo performance artist in a way that other people at my workplace wouldn't.

So I took the book home that weekend. On Saturday I read it in one day, cover to cover. On Sunday, I wrote a review on my new Apple Macintosh computer. Nobody told me to do this. I just decided to do it.

On Monday, I tentatively knocked on my boss' door.

"Nina?" I said.

"Yes?" she replied.

I summoned my courage. "Nobody asked for this, but I wrote a spec review of the Marilyn Manson memoir that releases this week. Here it is, if you'd like to run it."

I slid the book, with the review tucked inside, onto her desk. Nina King looked at it for a moment.

"Thank you," she said diplomatically.

I left her office quickly and returned to work. Then I waited.

It turned out that I didn't have to wait long. *The New York Times*, our archenemy, ran a review of the book two days later. That couldn't stand unanswered.

Michael Dirda came into my book room. "So good news—we're going to run that Marilyn Manson spec review that you submitted. You'll be paid four hundred dollars."

I can't remember what I said, but I'm sure it was gibberish. I was so happy I couldn't see straight.

"It was very well written," he added, then left.

That was the ultimate stamp of approval. I'm still proud of it, all these years later. Twenty-one years old, and a Pulitzer Prize-winning literary critic had complimented my writing. That was my literary fuel for years.

I had boldly stuck my head out of the hole, and someone important had draped a garland across it.

That same summer, I'd decided to write my first short story. I don't have a copy of it anymore, and I don't remember the title, but it was brief tale about a Muslim immigrant in the United States who abused his wife.

I don't know where the idea came from either. It just appeared to me, almost fully formed. I'd been reading *East, West* by Salman Rushdie, so maybe that played a role. Like Rushdie, I chose an ornate writing style. I'd also been reading Rick Moody and could have been imitating him as well.

I learned that the estate of F. Scott Fitzgerald was hosting a short story competition to celebrate the centennial of his birth. Without thinking about it, I photocopied the story, slid it into a big envelope, and mailed it to the estate.

Two months later, I received a telegram—a quaint mode of communication that I didn't know still existed—telling me that my story had received an honorable mention. It could've been something they told all the entrants, or maybe it was more selective. Either way, I held onto that small achievement for a few years. It sustained me too, when I felt my confidence ebbing.

Today, I don't care if my books ever hit bestseller lists. It's not a goal of mine. The reason is simple.

I used to compile The Washington Post's bestseller list.

Not every week, but occasionally. When the other assistant was on vacation, or if she was too busy, the task fell to me to assemble the list that appeared every week in the Style section. That task consisted of calling local bookstores and asking them to report to me a list of their bestsellers for the week, along with the number of copies sold. I looked for overlapping titles across stores and counted the sales numbers. The list consisted of 10 fiction and 10 nonfiction titles. Titles routinely made it onto that list with as few as fifteen copies sold.

So those types of lists may impress authors or readers who've dreamed about hitting them. But I worked behind the curtain. It was depressing to see how the sausage is made. Today, the New York Times doesn't even pretend to base its famous bestseller list on sales numbers: it has admitted that it often places its editorial thumb on the scale in favor of certain titles. It also refuses to disclose its exact methods.

My books will likely never be on a bestseller list (never say never). They will likely never have a great first week of high-velocity sales. But they will also never be remaindered—and they will quietly sell for decades, a few copies a month, with no promotion whatsoever. By the time I enter old age, they'll certainly have earned me a nice chunk of change and a decent readership.

This demonstrates how the produce model of traditional publishing—which views books as disposable properties that turn as rotten as bananas—is dead. We're in a new era of perpetual, long-term, independent publishing.

I'm perfectly happy with that.

I DID SPEAK up one more time during my six months at Book World.

The editors nicely invited me to sit in on a staff brainstorming meeting. I don't recall the specific topic, but I was happy to be welcomed into the fold. I do remember that it happened to occur on the morning that our newspaper broke the Monica Lewinsky scandal. The news editors upstairs had buried the explosive news in the seventeenth paragraph of a related White House story. The atmosphere in the hallways of the Post felt weird and skittery, as we'd breached journalistic decorum by suggesting the president had received oral sex from an intern.

It all seems so quaint now.

In this meeting, though, the editors were looking for new ideas about how to keep Book World relevant. I raised my hand.

"What if we partnered with that new bookselling website?" I said. "The one in Seattle."

"Which one?" someone said.

"Amazon dot com."

Amazon was an upstart that had recently made inroads into the world of bookselling. I'd already bought a couple books from it. It seemed like a natural thing to want to do. All publishing people were on the same team, right?

To my surprise, the staff all looked at me as if I had a cloud of maggots growing on my face. An uncomfortable silence fell upon the table. Someone changed the topic, quickly.

I said nothing more. Later, I understood: The Book World staff were fully in the pocket of traditional New York publishing. To them, Amazon was a disruptor to their normal distribution channels. It lay outside of the status quo, and therefore wouldn't be considered.

Fast forward a decade. In 2009, the Post executive team decided to close Book World as a separate Sunday section. Its few remaining reviews became scattered across different sections of the paper.

Then followed a chunk of irony big enough to choke a whale.

In 2013, the founder and CEO of Amazon, Jeff Bezos, purchased *The Washington Post* for $250 million. Under his ownership, the Post decided to reinstate the long-dead Book World section, in November 2022.

So they did end up partnering with Amazon in a different way, as I'd suggested over twenty years earlier, but in a very different way. It brought the entire Book World section back from the dead.

Over the next few months, I gained a few more bylines, and did some uncredited articles as well. I began to look around for next steps.

There weren't any.

The Post didn't promote from within, not since it had become so famous. To get onboard as a staff reporter or even as an intern, you needed reporting experience at two other daily newspapers first.

That was the rule, and I only knew of two exceptions. A Metro reporter had come onboard as an intern and had been so productive that they had no choice but to keep him. He'd filed nearly 400 articles in a single year. This guy was hugely obese, probably three hundred and fifty pounds, and looked stupid, so he was easy to underestimate. But his mind was razor-sharp. He was a real shark, and I admired him. The other exception was in the photo department: a young assistant had busted his ass taking thousands of photos on the weekends, for so long and for so well, that the photo department had decided to give him a staff position.

But working at two daily newspapers was asking a lot.

I'd already covered municipal debates and court cases while interning at a newspaper in Loudoun County, Virginia, a couple summers earlier, and it wasn't a good use of my time or skills. Why would I torture myself doing something I hated for the next five to ten years just to return to very newsroom where I was already working? Why would I sacrifice all my happiness to get bylines in the same newspaper where I'd already earned bylines?

That career was looking less like a ladder and more like a ring laying sideways. And I didn't want to take the time to run around it.

I'd thought about pursuing a magazine career, but that dream was quickly receding into the clouds, even in the late nineties, as freelancers watched their assignments vaporize. Mostly, I'd wanted to use journalism to vault into book publishing, the way Tom Wolfe had, but we'd been born fifty years apart, into very different journalism landscapes. Wolfe had made his name in the Sunday supplement magazines, which didn't even exist anymore. I couldn't do independent publishing yet, because vanity presses were a dirty word, and the book landscape hadn't yet been transformed. That wouldn't happen for another decade.

I'd also been watching the online environment, which was in its infancy. Like others, I saw bloggers provide good writing about niche topics. They were building their own audiences apart from traditional journalism. I saw the wave of information that advances in tech were bringing.

So I tried to suss out what was coming next. I looked into my crystal ball and saw a devastating period of transition for all legacy media, and for other traditional businesses too.

The ugly answer was staring at me in the face.

I had to leave.

It was another bold move, but I quit *The Washington Post*. Not angrily, not sadly. I did it quietly. I put in my notice, and they accepted it, as though they knew it had been coming.

True, I could've stuck around, picking up a paycheck, boasting to people that I worked at the Post. At the time, it impressed people in the nation's capital, and probably still does.

But that would've meant treading water, going nowhere. And we have just one life to live.

My last day came, and the book review staff bought me a cake and wished me well. I left the building with heavy feeling in my stomach. I kept my photo ID card as a token of my experience.

That was over a quarter century ago, and it was the last time I worked in journalism, or even published anything in a journalistic outlet. I retired from the field at age twenty three, after two summer internships, one four-year college newspaper career, and two years at *The Washington Post*.

At the time, some people thought I was crazy. To paraphrase Michael Crichton, who made a similar decision in the field of medicine, it felt like leaving the Supreme Court bench to become a bail bondsman.

But it was the right decision.

I've had a lot of failures in my life—you can read about some of them in *Strikethru*, the companion title to this one—but this wasn't one of them. It was a success. I studied the future, adjusted my plans, and acted without emotion. The way stock traders do.

Soon afterwards, Craigslist began stealing classified advertising from the newspaper business. For decades, classified ads had been the real backbone of local journalism, so this was devastating. Then Facebook was invented, and it vacuumed up news distribution across the country. Following that, predatory owners shuttered newspaper chains all over the country, selling them for parts. From 2008 to 2020, newspaper newsroom employment dropped 57%, from about 71,000 jobs to about 31,000. That figure doesn't include all the many losses in the ten years previous, nor does it include the many other losses since 2020 to the present.

If I'd tried to build a career in that environment, I would've failed. I would've been laid off, more than once. I would've become a resentful, alcoholic sack of misery.

Instead, I squeezed all the juice I could from that peach, then moved on. And slapping *The Washington Post* at the top of my resume for the next ten years opened many doors for me, especially while I was finding my footing. In fact, it's still on my resumé, but now closer to the bottom.

The Post taught me confidence in a workplace, confidence in my writing skills, and confidence in my ability to see my own future. I wouldn't trade that for anything.

8
THE HARD TIMES

I learned to be bold with women too—how to take charge while remaining playful.

If I liked a girl, and if we'd already met, I didn't wait to run into her somewhere. I would get her phone number, somehow, and cold call her for a date. The direct method worked. It felt a lot like journalism. Phone boldness was a real and necessary skill in the nineties, and it's disappeared. Young people today simply don't do it.

One girl I'd met was interning for conservative columnist Bob Novak at Crossfire, a popular CNN program. We chatted on a Friday, but I never got her number, so the next Monday I called her up at Novak's office and asked her out. She immediately said yes. Later, she told me that she'd said yes precisely *because* I'd had the stones to call her at work on Monday. We dated all that summer and have kept in touch over the years.

At my university, I'd known another girl named Anne for three years. I'd always felt a tiny bit of under-the-surface chemistry with her, and I also felt that she was a good person, so I asked her to join me for beer and nachos at a pub a couple blocks off campus. She hesitantly agreed. A few hours later, our lips met. Within a few weeks, we were a bona fide couple. Yes—I became one of the few men who have successfully broken themselves out of the friend zone. I'm still waiting for the ticker-tape parade for that one. Anne and I stayed together for nearly two years.

Many other girls turned me down, citing boyfriends who were impossible to verify. But the losses don't matter, only the wins.

I DECIDED TO WRITE A BOOK. It would be my first one. I'd never written anything longer than a short story, but that didn't stop me. I had an idea for a literary novel centered on the rave scene and trickster mythology.

Note that: *I decided*. Nobody told me to write a book. I had never done it before. I didn't know if it would be good. I used my freewill and made a choice to throw myself off the cliff.

To focus, I left Washington, D.C. and moved in with a friend who was finishing his master's degree at the University of Michigan. He needed a roommate for the last year of his classes. The rent was cheap and we both knew what we were getting with one another.

So I rented a truck and dragged all my stuff back to Michigan and into his place. I stayed seven months, typing like the wind. I had a good amount of savings but no income. I spent little money. I just made the dream happen, doing about 1000-1500 words per day. It felt like a lot then, but now 2000 to 3000 words per day is now my standard velocity as a professional.

When I finished, the manuscript clocked in at over

110,000 words, which was long. I spent another month making a shorter edit, close to 70,000 words. I settled upon a title: *Trickster*. I gave it to friends and family to read.

Their feedback was less than enthusiastic. No attaboys, no jokes about getting rich. A couple people never bothered to read it. Even my dad told me, "It's not as good as you think it is."

He was right. But I didn't know it yet.

I sent out fifty letters to fifty different agents. Seven requested partial or full manuscripts. Fourteen percent response was far above the querying average at the time. I mailed the heavy manuscripts, took author photos in advance, and waited.

The process was interminable: two months of twiddling my thumbs. I took a winter job at a brewpub just to bring some income. It taught me a lot about beer—dopplebocks, hefeweizen, amber ale, you name it. This place was at the leading edge of the craft beer movement. I soon isolated my favorite varieties: wheat beer in summer, and stout and porter in the winter.

Eventually, all the agents turned me down.

This effort wasn't useless. It resulted in what publishing calls a trunk novel. Meaning an early effort that's best kept in a trunk, locked away forever. I still have two copies of *Trickster*, but it lives in that proverbial trunk, never to see the light of day.

It was useful in the same way that tennis players return tens of thousands of serves. It's practice for when it counts.

Yes, I failed. And I needed to fail more and—as the saying goes—fail better.

I DECIDED to double down and write a second novel. This one I decided would be more ambitious, but it would also stick to famous American themes.

A road trip, a family, and Walt Disney World. These were the most mainstream topics I could think of.

Quickly I came up with a pilgrimage tale. A story of a dysfunctional family forced to undertake a journey to Orlando in order to win their dead mother's inheritance. I knew I wanted this to be a more professional effort, so I moved to central Florida to conduct some first-person research. I thought I would stay for six months, but it ended up taking me a year.

I got an evening job at a hotel, which left days and weekends free to do research on the history of central Florida at the Orange Country Public Library. I bought a Disney annual pass and visited the parks to take notes. Like a journalist, I chatted with Disney employees, trying to find out what life was like behind the orange curtain. I read everything I could relating to holy pilgrimages, family dysfunction, etc.

For a few months, I added an extra job selling timeshare condos at the Westgate Lakes Resort in Orlando. Most sellers were hired on commission, but the hiring manager liked me for some unknown reason and decided to pay me a small salary. Maybe he thought I could give 'em the old razzle-dazzle.

During the next three months, my insane daily schedule went like this: Arrive to the hotel for the night audit shift at 11 pm. Do the audit paperwork until 3 am. Sleep in an office chair for two hours. Wake up and steal some Krispy Kreme donuts that had been delivered for the café that morning. Help with early checkouts until 7 am. Leave hotel and drive to Westgate Lakes, eat a free sausage-and-egg breakfast at the buffet, sit down in the representatives' bullpen, and wait for the number on my greensheet to be called at around 9 am. Spend the next three hours touring the resort with a family. Unsuccessfully try to sell them a timeshare condo at the end of the tour. Drive home at noon. Be asleep by 2 pm. Wake up by 9 pm, and start over again.

The families came to take a tour of the resort in exchange for two free Disney tickets. Most of them would never buy, but a small percentage—less than ten percent—could be persuaded. Our job was to identify the ones who could be persuaded and drill them for gold.

I didn't think that I had a sales personality, but that wasn't totally true. It turned out that I was very good at building rapport. I was excellent at giving tours. I was strong at laying out the reasons for buying. But I was weak at asking for money at the end of the process.

I wasn't a closer, not at that time.

I only made one partial sale in three months, and when the bosses started sending my boss to ride along on my sales tours, I knew the end was near. I quit before I could be fired.

The timeshare experience taught me a few things. It taught me how to sell products. In a free market society like the United States, that should be a mandatory class in high school. It taught me assertiveness. Finally, it taught me when to recognize that your goose was cooked.

But I'd gone to Florida to write a second book.

With the extra job in my rearview mirror, and with the literary preparation all ready, I sat down and hammered out most of a draft in about two months. Next to my computer were some of my favorite novels: *All the King's Men* by Robert Penn Warren, *Bonfire of the Vanities* by Tom Wolfe, *The Grapes of Wrath* by John Steinbeck, *The Shining* by Stephen King. I consulted all of them for inspiration. I don't believe in the Great American Novel anymore, but back then I did—and I was consciously swinging for the fences.

By the time I finished, it clocked in at 100,000 words, about the same as the first novel. But I pushed myself too hard. I was living alone, and I felt like I was losing my mind. I needed to leave Florida and get on with my life, which I did.

It turned out that I wouldn't publish the book for years, not until after the independent publishing revolution began in 2010. But it has now seen the light of day. *When We Paid For Paradise* hasn't found much of an audience yet, but it was another step on the path. It taught me not to dwell on stories too much. I rewrote every sentence in that thing at least three times, which was a huge waste of time.

Today, with few exceptions, I scribble good first drafts, followed by a quick polish. And that's it.

9

THE NOT-SO-GREAT AMERICAN ROAD TRIP

Three months, thirty-nine states, and fifteen thousand miles of asphalt.

It was the ultimate summer road trip across the United States. I had ten thousand dollars, a tent, a sleeping bag, a map, a few travel guides, and a will to drive.

I also had a girl. Her name was Lilith, a blonde who'd just finished her master's degree at Johns Hopkins University and who wanted an adventure before she settled down to her new engineering job in California in the fall.

The only trope I didn't have was a sexy red convertible. Mine was a reliable gray Oldsmobile sedan inherited from my grandfather.

I too had decided to move to California later that year. I'd chosen to head to Los Angeles to pursue screenwriting opportunities. I knew that I would stay there for many years, so it was important to get some miles under my feet and adventure out of my system before hunkering down. There was a lot of the United States that I'd never experienced, including nearly everything west of the Mississippi.

Lilith and I traveled cheaply. For months, we slept in

campgrounds, cheap motels, and a lot of friends' couches. At university, Lilith had collected male admirers the way that other people collect stamps. She'd even made cute calendars of "the sexy men of the engineering department". Every state we visited, there was a different young engineering nerd waiting for us with an extra bedroom prepared. They always looked crestfallen at seeing me walk through the door. I don't think she'd told any of them about her male accomplice.

There were a lot of highlights. In the desert of west Texas, at Big Bend, we swam across the Rio Grande to Mexico and walked up a donkey path to a small *pueblito* for a beer at a concrete block shack. In southern Utah, we went two weeks without showering while clambering among the red rocks and slot canyons. In Oregon, we partied with radical leftists at a funk club. In the fields of Iowa, we stayed with a family of stodgy conservative farmers and challenged their boys to corn-on-the-cob-eating contests. And in Maine we spent a week in a large summer house with Lilith's extended family, right on the Atlantic coast, fifteen people I didn't know, all eating pots of clams for dinner and throwing bits of saltwater taffy into each other's mouths.

An entire summer of boldness.

―――

I ALSO LEARNED A BITTER LESSON: Vet your travel partners carefully.

See, I knew Lilith, but I didn't *know* her, if you get the distinction. Her behavior grew difficult as the weeks went on. I began to see emotional damage that she'd kept hidden since I'd met her a couple years earlier.

For one, she had no conflict-resolution skills. Lilith

started fights with no clear intention of ever concluding them. As a result, our disagreements would drag on for hours or days. Once, supremely annoyed, I dropped her off at a campground and left her there for five hours, alone. I don't apologize for that. She was acting that bad.

At other times, her anger and drama grew so prolonged that I would threaten to quit the journey completely. Eventually I discovered a terrible way to make her shut up: I talked in a soothing voice about how her father had abandoned her as a child. She would inevitably stop arguing, cry, and fall asleep. I don't apologize for doing that either. Manipulation was the only way to stop her madness.

Prior to the trip, two mutual friends had quietly warned me about her, but I'd brushed them off. This overconfidence hurt me. It wouldn't be the last time.

In retrospect, I'm mostly amazed at how little money we spent. The whole trip cost me about three thousand dollars total. That's a thousand dollars per month. I also was proud of the fact that I'd seized the moment. I thought I would never have this type of opportunity for extended travel again.

I was wrong about that—but I would wait fifteen years to find out.

A month after the journey ended, Lilith and I joined forces once again to share a moving van out to the West Coast. We argued most of the way, and after arriving in southern California, we immediately settled fifty miles apart and tried to forget about one another. When I saw her in person a year later, she admitted that she'd been "crazy" that summer (her word exactly). After that, she completely disappeared from my life.

Since then, a Google search tells me that she's become a visual artist focused on interpreting her trauma through oil and watercolor canvases. According to her biography at an art gallery, she is "haunted by memories of repeated childhood sexual assault" and "other abuse, too, by family and others". She never revealed any of that to me. At age twenty-four, I was unaware of just how many women are affected by sexual abuse. Today, I'm much more clued in. Today, I can spot the signs.

My three-month summer road trip was strong in bold ambition and planning, but flawed in its execution. I don't regret it—it gave me even more confidence to tackle nearly anything in life—but looking back, I would've chosen a different travel partner. I suspect Lilith might say the same about me.

10

A YOUNG CUB IN HOLLYWOOD

A few weeks before my twenty-fifth birthday, I arrived in Los Angeles with a single goal in mind.

I wanted to sell a feature film screenplay to a Hollywood production company.

It was a big dream, but it wasn't *that* big. I'd done my homework.

Think of screenwriting at that time as a giant iceberg: ninety percent of the paid writing that occurred never made it into production. There was a lot of churn in the market, and all of it was invisible to audiences. In fact, the Hollywood spec market for feature film screenplays had been red hot for over a decade. Writers you've never heard of became very wealthy in the nineties without ever seeing their work getting up on the screen. These writers sold spec screenplays, repeatedly, to different production companies, ranging from small (Alcon) to large (Miramax).

The money was good but not great. The sale of one script at WGA minimum—no frills, no actors attached—would net the writer about fifty thousand dollars after the ten-percent agency cut and taxes. That wasn't much. With time, and especially with a produced movie, a screenwriter could command a higher price. I knew of several writers with no credits who sold several scripts for half a million each. Their agents knew how to play producers off one another, creating buying frenzies and bidding wars. In addition, some screenwriters could also get lucrative rewrite assignments, which at the highest levels reached into the six figures for a single week of work.

Me, I just wanted to sell a single script. I knew it was a cutthroat business and kept my goals modest.

To SUPPORT MYSELF, I found a job analyzing screenplays for Fireworks Pictures. I got the job thanks to a friend of a friend who also worked there: we've lost touch, but she's become a senior executive at Paramount Pictures. I never thanked her properly. I also spent two days cold-calling other production companies in town, looking for work, which didn't pan out.

Fireworks Pictures had a minor hit with the slapstick comedy *Ratrace* around that time, starring John Cleese, Whoopi Goldberg, and others. Because of that success, they needed an extra set of eyes to handle the deluge of agented scripts that landed in their office every day. This was a couple years before the industry switched to emailed pdfs, so twice a week I drove to their Beverly Hills office in my new red Ford Ranger truck and picked up a heavy box filled with paper screenplays.

They paid me fifty or sixty dollars per script, more for a rush job. Each one took between two and three hours, so if I read quickly, it was decent money at that time. I worked in coffeeshops or at my dining room table. Over the next two or three years, I analyzed over nine hundred screenplays. I also judged a screenplay contest hosted by Madonna's production company, Maverick (which later went defunct and was revived by Guy Oseary as a management company).

Most of the stories I read were trash. Over and over, I analyzed scripts that displayed basic understanding of character, plot, pacing, dialogue, and theme. It got to the point where I could tell in five pages if it was a pass (terrible), a consider (very good), or recommend (excellent). Ninety-eight percent of what I read was a pass.

Frequently, the male writers lacked understanding of female nature. Other writers had no sense of conflict or plotting or escalating tension. For some reason, I read a lot of stories written by people having crises of conscience about homeless people. Personally, if I wanted to help homeless people, I wouldn't write a screenplay about them. I would volunteer at a shelter.

However, I did read a few excellent scripts before they were produced. *Akeelah and the Bee* (starring Keke Palmer, Laurence Fishburn, and Angela Bassett) was great on the page.

Another standout: a story about a twelve-year-old Muslim girl who wanted to play soccer like her hero, David Beckham. The script was terrific. An unknown 12-year-old actor named Keira Knightley was attached to star and the producers were looking for the final $1.5 million to complete their budget.

I recommended the script, something I almost never did. A week later, I popped my head into an executive's office at Fireworks.

"Hey Bob?" I said. "What did you think about that *Bend It Like Beckham* script?"

"It's not for us," he said.

"Why not?" I said. "You guys haven't made a movie in a year. There's nothing in the pipeline."

He shrugged. "We don't want to go in that direction."

He must've meant in the direction of success. *Bend It Like Beckham* was what they call a four-quadrant story: it appealed to males and females, young and old. Plus it had overlap with themes of conservative religion, which would appeal to India and the Middle East. And it used the name of the most famous athlete in the world at the time.

This was a slam dunk. And the investment was only one and a half million dollars—I knew the company could afford that. The return would at least keep the lights on.

I was proven correct. By 2020, the movie had earned $76 million on a less than $6 million budget, and it has become the highest grossing soccer movie in the history of cinema.

Meanwhile, two years later, Fireworks Pictures went out of business.

I'm not saying that I'm always right. But in that case, I was right. That's the fate of the professional Hollywood script reader. As an executive at James Cameron's production company once told me, "Oh you're a story analyst? You guys are the smartest people in any company, and we never listen to you."

Maybe he was flattering me, but I believed it. Anyways, the position is mostly gone now. As the feature film spec market dried up in the oughts, Hollywood stopped paying freelance story analysts. Any scripts sent by agents are now passed to unpaid interns to read over the weekends.

At the time, though, my neighborhood was an exciting place to work freelance. I'd settled into an apartment near 3rd and Robertson, an upscale area with the terrible name of Beverly Hills Adjacent. It was a small group of streets between Beverly Hills and West Hollywood, mostly known for expensive shopping, expensive lunches, and expensive medical care at Cedars-Sinai Medical Center.

Most days, after breakfast, I packed up my primitive Dell laptop and a couple of scripts and shuffled down the sidewalk past The Ivy (a famous place for People Who Lunch) to the intersection of Beverly and Robertson. There lay my destination: the Coffee Bean. A popular LA chain, the Coffee Bean is kosher and therefore is very popular on Saturday evenings with orthodox Jews as they break shabbat.

On a weekday morning, I typically chose one of their reading chairs and pulled out a large hardcover book of maps that I also carried with me. This was to protect my testicles from my computer. My Dell laptop weighed about eight pounds and it grew very hot and I was afraid it would affect my fertility. Other regulars probably assumed that I was the guy who loved maps so much he carried around a two-foot-wide hardcover collection of them. They wouldn't have been wrong. I do love maps, but I loved my sperm more.

This isn't a book about celebrities, but over five years I encountered hundreds of famous people parading through that coffee shop. It was fun. I chatted with Ozzy Osbourne about the state of the bathroom; he was unintelligible. I listened to an irritable Anthony Kiedis (vocalist for the Red Hot Chili Peppers) bicker with his girlfriend. I often saw Kiedis buzzing around the neighborhood on a lime-green

Vespa with a matching lime-green helmet. The late Matthew Perry (star of *Friends*) used to come in looking like death on a stick. I'm honestly surprised he lived as long as he did.

At night, I continued my cinematic education by watching different classic movies. Anything was fair game. *It Happened One Night, Sunset Boulevard, A Face in the Crowd, The Apartment, The French Connection, Reds*—I rented hundreds of them through a brand-new DVD-by-mail rental service that was starting to attract attention in the industry. It was called Netflix.

I also sacrificed television. For about five years, I didn't watch any television programs whatsoever. For young'uns reading this: Please know that television wasn't very good, not the way it is now, until about 2008. Other than *The Sopranos* and *Arrested Development*, which I caught years later, most programs were forgettable. I don't think I missed much of anything.

Since then, all this has changed. The best dramatic writing has gone to episodic television.

For fun, I liked to go mountain biking in the hills of Malibu with a friend from Michigan. On weekends, I'd go out with my first roommate, Noah, who was an excellent aspiring television writer. He had experience on sets and in writers' rooms and taught me a lot about storytelling. His problem was that he'd had a career as a business consultant for Boston Consulting Group prior to arriving in Hollywood, and at age twenty-eight he was considered too old even for a basic television sitcom writing job: he couldn't get hired anywhere. He wrote an excellent *Malcolm in the Middle* spec script that won a major award, but he never got any work off it. (The woman who won the same award a year earlier was given a staff job on *Frasier*.) Today, he lives in Atlanta and has returned to work as a business consultant.

Boldness and talent are both necessary, but in Hollywood, age and luck matter too.

I had a few favorite bars, like Boardner's in Hollywood, which was a World War II-era throwback with fantastic vibes. It had recently been used in a scene in *Ocean's Eleven* where Clooney and Pitt assemble the heist team. ("You think we need one more? You think we need one more.") In fact, I really enjoyed going out in Hollywood proper. I'm sometimes sensitive to people who've departed this earth, and I could feel the residual energy of the spirits of the dead on the streets there. It isn't a bad thing.

Mostly I favored St. Nick's Pub, a well-known (now-closed) joint with low mood lighting and good music. It was in my neighborhood—a block east of the gargantuan Beverly Center—so I could walk there, right down 3rd Street, and stumble back home at the end of the night. People were friendly in there, especially Marlon Chavarria, the veteran bartender who was later killed in a car accident. He was a sweet guy. It was a casual, no-frills watering hole where most people liked to end their evenings, but I often started and ended there.

There, I once struck up a conversation with a girl who worked at Jimmy Buffett's management company. Jimmy Buffett was a billionaire musician and entrepreneur who built his empire on some wobbly songs about drinking tequila and sailing boats. They had titles like "Margaritaville" and "It's Five O'Clock Somewhere".

"Jimmy Buffett," I said, furrowing my brow. "Can I ask you a weird question?"

"Sure," she said.

"I don't mean to be insulting, but who listens to Jimmy Buffett? I've never known any fans."

"Alcoholics," she replied.

Her face was utterly serious. This wasn't a joke.

"Really," I said.

She nodded. "Our audience lives mostly in trailer parks and they save up their money to see Jimmy once a year, every summer. We've built our business around them."

I never forgot that. It was my real-world introduction to the concept of identifying your audience and market segmentation.

FOR A FEW MONTHS, I took an assistant job at a literary agency representing Hollywood screenwriters. It was called Origin, and it's been closed for years now, absorbed by bigger fish in the sea. My job was simple: run the copy room, keep the Xerox machine going, make deliveries, occasionally answer a phone, and basically do whatever people needed.

The reason I took this job, despite being hugely, massively, ridiculously overqualified, was to learn the business and meet some agents. I did both. I got to know the business, and I met nine different agents. But they took no interest in me.

I'd never seen Hollywood agents up close before. The partners of Origin were an interesting group. One was Michael, a gay connoisseur of the visual arts, who kept curiously asking my opinion about his newest purchases. Another, Thomas, had an anger management problem; he used to rip paper to shreds after stressful negotiations with studio executives. For some reason, Thomas liked me, and he invited me to stay for staff meetings at his exquisite home off Mulholland Drive, high in the Hollywood Hills.

The principal partner, Benjamin Scheff, didn't like me hanging around at those meetings. He didn't like me, period. He didn't like his own executive assistant either, despite her twenty years of loyalty to him. He didn't like anybody—never have I encountered a more disagreeable piece of shit than Benjamin Scheff. Psychology experts always say you should trust your intuition, and my skin crawled whenever he was near.

The feeling was mutual, because he eventually fired me for no reason. I could've sued him, but it was a Hollywood firing. Meaning that it was pointless. It happens all the time with the temperamental trolls of the entertainment industry. You just accept it and move on. The damaged people of Hollywood love to take petty revenge upon the world that wronged them as children.

A junior lit agent there, Naha, was about my age. She was clever but green, a bit girly, a little unsure of herself. Now and then she used to ask me to drive her somewhere in my truck. I had a bit of a crush on her because she was beautiful, and she was my type. Once she came to work wearing nothing but a gray bodysuit, red flats, and a pearl necklace. I still haven't forgotten that image. Today, Naha has become a top agent at CAA and a serious Hollywood power player. She's represents A-list names and has been instrumental in some of biggest deals in the world of global entertainment. I'm happy for her stratospheric success, though I didn't see it coming. However, she likes to talk about Palestine a lot, which is a problem in an industry filled with Jews.

I did one embarrassing thing there. I discovered that Elite Modeling Management had their LA offices right down the hall from this agency. As a young single guy, I had a sudden idea. I collared the mailman one day and asked him to start placing one piece of Elite's mail into my agency's mail. This would give me a daily excuse to go down the hall, knock on their door, and be welcomed into a Valhalla filled with exquisitely beautiful young women in lingerie having ecstatic pillow fights. At least that's how I pictured it.

The mailman laughed and agreed.

The piece of Elite mail came the next day, but the ruse backfired. Inside the modeling agency, I only found a severe middle-aged woman in a black blouse and her frantic male assistant. The models were nowhere to be seen. In fact, the girls never came into the office at all. Then I couldn't find the mailman to tell him to stop the trick, so I ended up delivering extra mail to those two for a few weeks.

While pursuing all these ambitions, I went without health insurance for five or six years. This was a risk that paid off, but it was a risk I would rather not have taken.

In the United States, freelancers like myself used to have no good options for health insurance, since insurance plans were (and still are) often tied to full-time W2 employment.

I could've paid massive amounts of money for an individual plan, but that seemed unnecessary to me. I was in tip-top health, always had been. My life was urban and safe, except for occasional camping trips into the deserts or the forests of California. I wasn't even mountain biking anymore, not since my new thousand-dollar bike had been stolen off my second-floor balcony by agile thieves.

If anybody was going to gamble and live without health

insurance, it was me. My reasoning was that all the money I would save would eventually outweigh any out-of-pocket medical service I might hypothetically need.

It worked out. I didn't so much as stub a toe, and later I found health insurance through my ill-fated first marriage. But nobody in a developed country should go without health insurance the way I did.

A few years later, I volunteered for Barack Obama's 2008 presidential campaign for one big reason—his promise to rectify this. He and the Democrats did exactly that. They fixed some of the health insurance gaps in the first year of his first term. I've been enrolled in the Health Insurance Marketplace ever since.

Despite living in the center of the visual storytelling world, and analyzing screenplays all day, I hadn't studied story structure very closely.

My bachelor's degree was in literature, but I'd only taken courses in old poetry and the history of the novel. At some point, I realized that studying *Tristram Shandy*, written by a seventeenth-century Irish cleric, wasn't going to help me sell a comedic screenplay or publish mystery-thriller novels in the twenty-first century. My master's degree was in rhetoric and composition, which was very beneficial later, when I moved into education, but it served no purpose in the hallways of Paramount or Warner Brothers.

So I swallowed my pride and went back to school.

I signed up for a UCLA Extension class in comedic screenwriting. It was taught by Stephen Mazur, an experienced screenwriter who had written *Liar, Liar*, among other movies. In a small classroom setting for the first time in many years, I learned that there was little difference between comedy and drama on the page. Tone was determined by actors, directors, and cinematographers, not by writers. Stephen showed me how to break down a story into sequences—not scenes, but collections of scenes with individual arcs. He demonstrated how most popular stories follow an eight-sequence structure, whether the authors intended it or not.

That last piece of knowledge was a huge breakthrough. I've never stopped using the eight-sequence structure, not even after sixty books and thirty screenplays. It applies to novels just as easily as to films. Today, my wife and I sometimes talk shop in terms of sequences. "Hey babe, how's your book going?" "It's okay—I'm on sequence six, but I don't think the dark moment is dark enough."

My writing immediately improved. I wrote a third novel, based on a previous screenplay, called *Hysterical For Harvard*. It was the best thing I'd written at that point. I also wrote a couple of screenplays that did get some momentum. One, *John School*, was a comedy about a young groom who is sentenced to attending a school for johns (people busted for soliciting prostitutes) on the same day as his wedding. It ended up as a finalist in a top screenwriting competition, but it didn't go anywhere after that.

If I hadn't admitted that I still needed to learn, I wouldn't have reaped later benefits.

11
DATING IN LA: HOT PEOPLE, COLD CONNECTIONS

I had zero luck with women during my first year in Los Angeles.

My background was in liberal arts and newspaper journalism. I'd gone to Oxford University. I'd written two books. I come from a moderate Midwestern family.

None of this mattered in Los Angeles.

My problems were legion. The "mattresses" (model-actresses) who surrounded me didn't value the creative or intellectual assets that I'd built up in my life. They valued a wealthy and connected man—period.

I had emotional self-awareness, but that was worth less than an ice cream cone. I was tall and good-looking, but that meant nothing either, not in a city packed full of tens of thousands of other tall and good-looking men, all trying to get roles on a sitcom. Socially, I often had to explain to strangers that I wasn't an actor. "I'm a writer," I would say. That was a small advantage. In the Hollywood pecking order, we writers are viewed a bit more positively than desperate actors.

In fact, after spending so much time around hopeful actors, I began to feel sorry for them. Actors are the unlicked cubs of the Hollywood ecosystem. Many in LA are open wounds using staged drama as a way to address their own childhood traumas. Most people view them with pity or derision, unless they somehow are either very lucky (the cast of *Friends*) or very superb (Ian McKellen). Then they're rewarded, which probably screws them up even more. The best a Hollywood hopeful can usually aim for is to become what's known as a working actor: someone who makes enough to pay the bills, but who remains unknown.

Most young women in my area were trying to gain a foothold in the business. After sizing me up, they accurately guessed that I was a minnow in the great studio food chain. Predictably, they would lose interest, in a matter of weeks, days, hours, or even minutes. Love is very transactional in that part of that city.

In short, I was selling winter coats at the beach in August. Nobody was buying.

My wife has told me that I would've had a very different love story if I'd never gone to Los Angeles. I would've found a solid, dependable woman much sooner, someone who valued my qualities and assets, someone who respected men. I did eventually find her, but only in my mid-forties, on a faraway island in the Caribbean.

Still, that weird Los Angeles entertainment ecosystem filled something in me. In the words of Bono, the lead singer of U2, I needed to "slide down the surface of things". I'd spent so long searching for meaning in written texts that sometimes I wanted nothing to matter very much. I was searching for shallowness. The first U.S. poet laureate, Robert Penn Warren, said at the end of his life that he felt relieved that he no longer felt the desire to write poetry, or to look for deeper meaning. I understand that relief very well.

In the meantime, I had a lot of dates that went nowhere. There was a weird two-week flirtation with Leonard Cohen's daughter, who it turned out was totally mental. There was a pair of unsuccessful dates with a producer of the movie *Idiocracy*: I guess we wanted to make doubly sure that we were wrong for one another. I made a long drive to Redondo Beach to meet with a redhead who worked in an autism clinic, who sent her friends to meet me instead. I met a schizophrenic girl on disability whose face was perpetually frozen in a flat affect. I started to fall for an attractive pub waitress who was also a writer, like me, but who was so unhappy with her life that she rendered herself undateable.

That was all just the first year.

In a city of twelve million people, you can go on dozens of terrible first dates. I did exactly that—over eighty of them, if memory serves. The gorgeous vegan yoga teacher actress who'd had a role on an episode of *Seinfeld* (I never learned which one) who was obsessed with numerology and told me that my birthdate made me a portal to another dimension. I ended that date after twenty minutes, beauty be damned.

Or the Vietnamese girl who showed up for our date with a large cat on a leash. It was a half wild African cat, a queen, and she was breeding it for profit. After coffee, she suggested taking the animal for a walk. I ended up pulling it out of trees, hauling it out of sewers, and dragging it across lawns and driveways. Later I discovered the girl had a message on her answering machine saying, "Herpes is like a box of chocolates, you never know what you gonna get." We hadn't done anything in that department yet, and I quickly saw myself to the exit.

In a way, every one of those dates was a small risk, a step into the unknown. I was putting myself out there, casting the net, seeing what I wanted to catch and what I wanted to release. Most were released quickly.

The only thing at stake was my pride. That was something I had no shortage of.

12
MT. WHITNEY: THE LONGEST DAY

I did take one huge physical risk in Los Angeles. I climbed Mt. Whitney in a single day.

Located in the Sierra Nevada mountains of central California, Mt. Whitney is the tallest mountain in the contiguous 48 states, topping out at 14,500 ft (4421 m). The trail runs for almost 11 miles each way (about 22 miles total) and goes a mile and a half straight up into the sky. It can be finished in a single day, an exhausting non-technical climb that starts at about 7500 feet (2286 m).

I decided to try it.

I persuaded a close friend, Brian, to do it with me, and we won a lottery for day passes in June. We trained on other mountains in the weeks leading up to the climb. First was a short climb to summit Mt. Baldy, where we passed bighorn sheep and learned how to pace ourselves. The tortoise beats the hare, every time, on the side of a mountain. Two weeks later, we practiced on a longer one: we summited Mount San Gorgonio, a.k.a. Old Grayback, where we stumbled into a California condor, the largest bird in North America. Critically endangered, it was shockingly huge, a massive black thing with a wingspan of at least nine feet. My nose was taken aback by its dark, rank, primitive scent.

On the weekend of the Whitney climb, Brian and I drove up to the Owens Valley in my truck a couple days early, containers of premade rice and pasta bouncing around in the bed. We spent time acclimating to the high altitude in gorgeous mountain meadows. I brought folding chairs and books. We swallowed huge amounts of starch and sunned ourselves and inhaled and exhaled deeply and enjoyed a pause from our busy lives.

The hike itself was harder than I'd supposed, even with preparation. Our alpine start began at four o'clock in the morning. My headlamp lit up the rocky dirt trail in front of my feet. Eventually the sun rose, and the trail steepened. At nine o'clock am, we broke for lunch—bagels and sliced ham—at the edge of a gorgeous alpine lake. We were at 12,000 feet (3657 m) and I hadn't felt any effects of altitude yet.

The worst segment of the trail came after that. The 99 Switchbacks is the most infamous section of the Mt. Whitney hike. Surrounded by nothing but granite—we'd already passed the treeline far below—we carried ourselves up nearly 2000 feet (600 m) of elevation in about two miles of trail. It's crazy. Picture yourself going straight up the wall of a skyscraper that itself has been built two and a half miles high in the sky. That's what it was like.

I saw piles of vomit on the trail, small gifts from previous hikers. Despite the fact that we were simply walking, I'd never felt so gutted and worn out. The altitude began to take its toll on me. I thought about the deaths that occurred on this trail, usually one each year. According to a park ranger, the most common victim was an overweight desk jockey who suffered a heart attack while pursuing his dream.

At the top of the switchbacks, Brian and I paused for photos. This was 13,800 feet (4200 m). At sea level, the air is about 20 percent oxygen; here, it was only 12 percent. We crossed the Notch, a narrow spit of land with thousand-foot falls on either side. It's treacherous. I'd been advised to cross on hands and knees, which I did.

After that, we stumbled through eerie fields of scree that resembled the surface of Mars. We had to stop every couple hundred feet to catch our breath. I questioned my own judgment for having suggested this ludicrous climb.

On the final approach to the summit, I started crying. It surprised me because I almost never cry. In fact, as I type this, I haven't fully cried in seventeen years. Up there, near the top of Mt. Whitney, I didn't feel sad, or happy, or anything—just exhausted from being so determined. My body dealt with the stress by releasing tears.

After nine hours, we finally arrived at the summit. It was a surprisingly placid place, with other hikers stretched out on the rocks, sunning themselves in the UV rays. I found a pit toilet built into the rocks nearby and dropped my pants while Brian took a photo of me sitting on the highest can in the country. Then we took off our boots and enjoyed a celebratory Gatorade.

After an hour's rest, we changed shirts and began the descent. Almost immediately, Brian began to grow ill. It was altitude sickness. Surprisingly, it had waited to ambush him until now, on the descent. We'd talked about this possibility beforehand and assumed that it was likely to hit one of us.

Soon Brian was puking on the trail. His pace slowed. He had other embarrassing problems that I won't go into; use your imagination. I helped him all the way, slowing down our pace, waiting for him during the rests, knowing he would've done the same for me. The sun arched overhead and crashed into the western horizon. By eight o'clock pm we were in blackness once again—and we were still miles from the portal where we'd started.

Finally, at one o'clock in the morning, Brian and I arrived at the trailhead and beelined directly for our tent. It had been twenty-one hours of hiking. We'd burned around ten thousand calories. We fell into our sleeping bags on the hard ground and passed out for nine straight hours.

The next morning, Brian woke up feeling great, like he'd never been sick. My body, on the other hand, felt as though it'd been beaten with sandbags.

Back in Los Angeles, in the days that followed, we tried to get a handle on our feelings about the climb, and about the future. It took a while to process. I wasn't sure if I wanted to climb the mountain again, at least not for a long time. Brian felt like *never* was the better answer. I suggested a different idea: what if we made a pact to climb it together once a decade? I considered him my best friend at the time, and we were twenty-seven years old. We could climb it at age thirty-seven, forty-seven, fifty-seven, etc. It could be a way to mark the passage of our lives and our sure-to-be life-long friendship as well. We'd been buddies for fifteen years already, and I was positive that it wouldn't ever stop.

We decided to table that decision.

Two years later, our friendship ended, and I never climbed the mountain again.

It's better this way. As the Japanese say, a wise man climbs Mt. Fuji once, but only a fool climbs it twice.

13

THE TEFLON DRINKER

So far, I've had about 25,000 alcoholic drinks in my life.

Many people say that drinking alcohol is a gamble with your health, but I've been drinking nightly for over twenty years with no ill effects.

I didn't always drink. In fact, I started it a bit later than other people.

In high school, I never touched the stuff. I stayed that way in my first year of college, when half the monkeys on my dormitory floor were getting soused five nights a week. In my second year of college, I broke my discipline and drank twice. In my third year, I discovered beer after arriving at Oxford University, where I was legal to order at the pubs, and where the English tipple was like golden rays of sunshine slipping down your throat. The famous English brand Boddington's was so good on tap that it ruined me for American beer for years afterwards.

Later, in my mid-twenties, I only drank outside the house. It was a social ritual for me, and I had all the usual drunken nights that twentysomethings enjoy. Mostly I chose liquor. I hadn't found wine yet, and the craft beer revolution was only in its infancy. I don't have many crazy drinking stories like most people do, except for once passing out inside an Oscar Meyer Wienermobile, which had been left unlocked overnight. That was fun.

At age thirty, I discovered California wines, and that kickstarted a two-or-three-glass a night habit that's still ongoing. I started to drink at home, often alone. They say that's something you're not supposed to do, but it works fine for me.

It's true that some people can't handle alcohol. For them, it causes loss of impulse control and releases the worst goblins hiding inside the caves of their psyches. But my skull is free of monsters. The worst thing to emerge was the small people-pleaser who used to hang out there. In fact, some people said I acted like a game show host after a few drinks. Fine: so be it. I can think of worse things. That people pleaser has now been evicted anyways.

In my forties, I've known or read about people my age quitting alcohol completely. These people say it improves their sleep. They say it gives them better mental clarity. They say it improves their relationships with people around them. They say it helps them avoid divorce court and child custody battles. John Mayer says quitting booze elevated his entire life.

For them, I don't doubt that's true. But I seem to be built different. Red wine or gin on the rocks helps put me to sleep. It brings me down, late at night, when this night owl still has a bit too much energy. My mental clarity is the same either way, maybe because my tolerance is so high—I barely feel a glass or two of whiskey these days. And alcohol has always been irrelevant to the quality of my relationships.

I drink for other reasons you wouldn't expect. In cold

weather climates, I drink to warm myself up. At home in the winter, I like to make hot whiskey toddies to stay warm and fight off impending colds. Downhill skiing, too: I was shown the beauty of a nip of Grand Marnier while on a ski lift.

Genetics plays a role. My family seems to metabolize alcohol well. My parents have been throwing back two or three drinks a night for the last fifty or sixty years. If my math is correct, they've each put away well over a hundred thousand alcoholic drinks in their lives, almost all brandy, whiskey, and vodka. This habit has never affected them, either for good or bad. In fact, my father himself is a retired drunk driving defense attorney who spent part of his career handling alcoholics. I can remember the phone occasionally ringing early on Sunday morning, yet another client who'd ended up in the slammer a few hours earlier. *Goddamn it man, get sober*! he once shouted.

I do go without alcohol sometimes. A week in Saudi Arabia forced me to go dry, except for what they call a "Saudi cocktail"—apple juice with lemon-lime soda. In 2024, I put all booze aside for several weeks while fighting dengue fever. Occasionally, I'll do a few dry and sugarless weeks in January after the excesses of the holiday season. In Barbados, my wife's homeland, the poncha crema, dark rum, rum punch, rum cake, and rum cookies can overwhelm your liver if you're not careful.

In short, my body feels like an ocean liner. You can throw a few bottles of beer at its sides, spill a bottle of wine on the deck, or break a bottle of champagne across its bow. None of it really matters much. The ocean liner is still headed forward. This isn't braggadocio: it's my lived experience.

While the quantity of my intake is probably the riskiest thing that I do, there are factors mitigating that risk. I'm a muscular male who weighs 220 lbs (98 kg), and I have a long history of healthy imbibing. I exercise a ton, which forgives a lot of bodily abuses as well. And years ago, my low HDL numbers led my doctor to recommend drinking a bit more, since that can raise good cholesterol. (It did, from 39 up to 66.)

Reformed alcoholics like to say that if you're ever asking if you're drinking too much, you probably are. That's not true. I've asked myself the question, studied my liver and kidney numbers on my blood panels, and decided to stay the course.

At least for now.

14

THE VOWS WERE LIES

Rolling the dice on a big life decision is inherently dangerous. Do it enough times, you're going to lose one badly, and suffer the consequences.

By age thirty, I'd taken a lot of big risks, and all of them had turned out either wins or draws. But no real losses. Subsequently, I was flying high. I wasn't getting rich, but I was progressing in many other avenues. In a way, I felt bulletproof.

Then I married a bad person. In my family, we now call her Fang, a nickname given by my sister to describe my ex-wife's vibe.

In my defense, I was partly duped by her. In our first two years together, up through the engagement, Fang hid from me the worst parts of her own personality. Then, about two months before the wedding, she pulled back the curtain, unleashing the hounds of dysfunction. She revealed the emotional dysregulation that she'd taken special pains for me never to see during our courtship.

Her behavior grew so bad that I dragged her to a couples' therapist to find out what was going on in her head.

The sessions didn't yield many answers, but the therapist noted that he'd like to meet with her privately, to probe a bit more. She never went.

You can read a lot more about this flaming trash fire of a marriage in *Strikethru*, a history of my failed relationships. I briefly mention it here because this was another risk—one that failed, badly.

In hindsight, the reason for my failure now seems obvious.

I was overconfident.

It's the white man's weakness. Despite the signals that popped up throughout the two-and-a-half-year courtship, and the flurry of red flags that sprang up in the two months before the wedding, I was convinced that I knew enough about women to take control of the marriage. I felt I could make it work. I told myself that with enough willpower, I could straighten her out, make her see reason, and bring her to heel. (Yes, that's dog training language, chosen on purpose.)

But this was a mistaken belief. And it came from my too-strong belief in myself.

A person can only change if she recognizes that a change is necessary. Fang saw nothing wrong with herself. She was perfectly happy being a materialistic shopping addict with a penchant for self-glorification. Her strongest and only belief was in her own superiority.

Years later, listening to Donald Trump blather on about his imaginary victories, I sometimes would be struck by the similarities between them. It gave me the shivers. How could I have married someone like that?

Earlier I wrote that, at this point in my life, I could've used some humbling. Well, this experience gave me a triple dose of humility. Over the five years of our marriage, I learned that you can't fix crazy, that emotional dysregulation is unsolvable by outsiders, and that narcissistic personality disorder is a real thing that has no endgame except the destruction of the relationship.

There was nothing I could do to change any of it. I took a risk, and I got burned. Here's what it cost me:

1. **Emotionally**. Fang tried her hardest to emasculate me, using insults, criticisms, and manipulation. I saw her doing it, recognized what she was doing, and was able to fight her off by standing up for myself. But it wasn't easy.
2. **Financially**. When she finally walked out, I was still paying off fifteen thousand dollars of her credit card debt—in addition to paying our nearly two-thousand-dollar rent. She made slightly more money than me in the last two years of our relationship, and yet the lion's share of the bills fell upon my shoulders. According to her lying math, we were somehow even. I haven't forgotten that. It was Trumpian logic.
3. **Physically**. Her endless pokes, jibes, insults, and mockery weakened my immune system. My normally healthy body began contracting upper-respiratory illnesses four to five times a year, and my coughing lasted for weeks. Like any good wife, she viciously berated me for my illnesses, which made them even worse.

It sounds bad, and it was. But I don't want to overstate things. Once the marriage was finally dragged behind the barn and put out of its misery, I bounced back quickly.

Physically, I took it easy that year—no weightlifting, no

sprinting, no high-intensity exercise at all. I allowed my body to recuperate. I only jogged, bicycled, and swam, plus some easy yoga.

Financially, we had shared nothing, and we wanted nothing from one another, so it was an easy split. I forced her to pay for all the filing fees and paperwork, since ending the marriage had been her idea. In that way, I made her take emotional ownership of the process. The entire divorce process cost me a total of three dollars, for photocopies and postage.

But the emotional recuperation was the longest and heaviest process. Recovering from mild narcissistic abuse is a serious thing, no matter how strong or independent you fancy yourself to be, and it took nearly two years before I felt like myself again. Even then, I knew that the experience had changed me.

15

FLUENT IN CONFUSION

For years, I hated the Spanish language. Other than Raisin Bran—which sends me into irrational spasms of rage—it was the bane of my existence.

I had zero early exposure to any foreign language. I never heard a word of Spanish until college. There, I took four required semesters, taught by four different professors from four different parts of the world—Chile, Puerto Rico, Spain, and Mexico.

It killed me.

Classroom instruction, it turned out, is a terrible way to acquire a foreign language. I'm a contextual learner, which is a fancy way of saying that I need to be immersed in the place where it's spoken.

This handicap was revealed in all its ugliness in my third college class, Spanish 203. The professor was an arrogant prick from Madrid who carelessly assigned hundreds of subjunctive verbs for nearly a month straight. He was terrible at explaining the conjugations too. He couldn't be bothered. At the time it wasn't even clear that we were making the switch to the hypothetical.

I began failing exams. During the in-class mock conversations, which were also graded, I couldn't cope, barely forming sentences. My grade sank further. The professor offered no help to any of us; he seemed unconcerned by suffering. I was a full-scholarship student, so the curse of high expectations made my failure feel even worse.

My final grade in Spanish 203 was a C. That was his gift, I believe. Even today, it remains the only C of my life.

After finishing the final class, I ceremonially burned all my Spanish notes, books, and materials in a bonfire at the beach. That's how much I despised it. I felt free at last, free at last, thank God almighty.

THEN THE UNIVERSE took its revenge upon me.

A year later, I discovered that I needed to pass a foreign language qualifying exam to earn my master's degree. I had no choice but to return to my bitch mistress. And I'd burned all my materials in a pit.

I had to start from scratch. I spent the next six months teaching myself Spanish on paper, using children's books, workbooks, anything I could find. I practiced at lunch, on the subway, at my desk at The Washington Post.

On my first attempt, I failed the equivalency exam by a mere ten points. I studied more and went back to the testing room a few weeks later. The test administrator handed me the test book and said, "It's the same test you took before."

I looked at it. It was literally the same exam. They just kept it in a drawer and pulled it out when someone needed it.

This time, I passed by ten points.

The next summer, I burned all my notes for a second time. I was truly finished with Spanish.

You would never expect that person, over twenty years later, to become fully fluent in Spanish, or to become fascinated by the cultures that support it, or to be able to passionately explain the minute differences in the diction and syntax from country to country in Latin America.

You would never expect that person to spend a year and a half of his life in South America.

You would never expect that person to write several novels set deep inside Latin American and Spanish culture.

But I did those things. I changed—and what changed me was that C grade.

There are certain things we know we will never excel at. For me, it's gymnastics and botany. But my soul told me that I could be good at Spanish. I'm verbal—I think and speak and write fast—and I didn't like falling on my face so badly. It felt like I'd been cheated in a rigged competition.

It would take many years before I could prove that to myself.

I returned to the Spanish language in my thirties. Together with my disaster of an ex-wife, who partly came from Puerto Rican blood, I began traveling to Latin America for adventures.

I could speak some basic sentences, but I couldn't understand anybody at all. Fang, on the other hand, was frightened of speaking—she couldn't tolerate the thought of being seen as less than perfect. But her Puerto Rican grandmother had yelled at her in Spanish for years, so she understood it well.

I was the mouth, she the ears. Together, we muddled our way through two different trips to Argentina and Uruguay. To me, they stand as highlights of our relationship, the happiest days we ever had. We also visited her extended family in Puerto Rico for ten days and toured the island. For our honeymoon, we took three weeks in Spain.

None of these trips were guided. We did them all solo.

I slowly grew addicted to Latin culture. I listened to classic tango of Carlos Gardel and Astor Piazzolla. We ate in the Argentine and Peruvian and Spanish restaurants of Los Angeles. I devoured travel magazines and travel blogs and books such as *The Open Veins of Latin America*, by Eduardo Galeano. And I wrote novels set in Latin America: the Ainsley Walker Gemstone Travel Mystery series, which quickly found an audience.

Still, I knew that I would never grow fluent unless I found a way to spend at least three months immersed in Latin America. Given my constantly busy work schedule, I couldn't afford to do that. Plus, my married life, the one I'd chosen and made for myself, made it impossible. So that dream would have to die.

But I made one mistake.

I assumed that I would always be married to Fang.

THE END CAME SWIFTLY. The writing appeared on the wall in December, and by the first week of February, she'd walked out. (Read about our relationship in more detail in the companion memoir, *Strikethru*.)

Alone in my apartment, I made plans for my future.

I knew immediately that I wouldn't stay in Los Angeles. I'd been chafing at the limits of the city for a few years, and now I was free to flee. I knew that I would move to Chicago, my favorite city in the United States. I'd been visiting the Windy City for my entire life and had hoped to live there someday.

Before relocating, though, I decided to spend several months in South America. It was the perfect joint in my life. In this way, I would finally become fluent in Spanish. I would date a lot of beautiful Latin women. I would stop working so hard for a while. All three goals were interconnected.

How many months exactly? That wasn't clear. I bought a plane ticket to Medellín, Colombia. I didn't buy a return ticket because I didn't know when I'd be coming back.

16

STARTING OVER IN SOUTH AMERICA

Buying a one-way ticket to South America sounds like the last-ditch effort of a man at the end of his rope.

I get that. From the outside, it does sound like I was throwing in the towel on life, trying to salvage my soul. That wasn't right, but it wasn't totally wrong either. Mostly, I just needed a sabbatical. It's not every day that your legally wedded spouse sticks up her middle finger at you and walks out on your marriage, for no reason. I decided to take time to myself, lick my wounds, and rebuild something new.

———

I chose to begin my adventure in Medellín, Colombia. I stayed in a fourteenth-floor narco-penthouse that I found on Airbnb. It's no longer available for rent, but at the time it featured eight bedrooms and a huge main living area with pool table, sofas, wide-screen televisions, and communal kitchens. It was basically a swanky group home for male gringo tourists. The double-reinforced bulletproof front door and 360-degree balcony also hinted at its defensive use during the Escobar era. We learned that the original owner of the building had been gunned down several years earlier in the Poblado area of the city.

To me, it was like being dropped into a wild animal exhibit. Some of the men who were staying there during my first month were flat-out degenerates. One guy, Dave, a fifty-five-year-old former military man from Wisconsin, was a full-on sex addict. He brought three to four hookers a day into the penthouse, and got upset if any of them arrived late, because it ruined his scheduled bookings for the day. I rode in the elevator with a couple of the girls, and let's just say it was clear to me that he wasn't checking IDs. Dave was a broken soul.

Another guy, Sam, was a long-haul trucker who'd been badly disfigured in an accident. His brain had been damaged too, and the hookers he brought into the penthouse sometimes fled screaming after his bizarre sexual requests involving bodily fluids. A third guy, a former boxer, stayed there while recovering from a hair transplant operation. Colombia is very good for affordable elective surgery.

Then there was Kevin, was struggling with mental health issues; he loved to drop acid and walk through the city throwing Frisbees. Once, he wandered off a tour of downtown, and I spent an hour roaming the criminal alleys of El Centro looking for him. That was the most dangerous hour of my entire life. Word of advice to all readers: don't do dumb shit in South American cities, especially if you're a gringo like him with pasty white skin and a fondness for cargo shorts. Sometimes I wonder if Kevin is still alive. I give it fifty-fifty odds.

Another guy was a scammer from Toronto who told the other guests that he could get them free flights on a private airplane courtesy of the famous music label he used to work at. A couple of the more gullible guys stupidly handed him five hundred dollars each, and that was the last they ever saw of that money: the scammer fled one night, with their cash, and was never heard from again.

A well-behaved young Christian couple from the United States arrived at the penthouse one Friday afternoon. I felt sorry for the woman, because I knew how insane things could get over the weekend. (Medellín has a strict Thursday-to-Saturday party culture.) I chatted with her and tried to put her at her at ease, but things degenerated as usual, and she looked petrified the last time I saw her. They left quickly on Sunday morning.

One night, a fiftysomething white American guy entered our penthouse. He was staying in a different part of the city and had great, positive energy. I liked him immediately. He introduced himself as Tom from Tallahassee, and we chatted for part of the night, taking pointless hits on a vape pen and discussing life in Colombia. I felt like I'd found a kindred spirit.

After he left, I turned to my housemates. "He was a really nice guy."

There were some smirks. "You know what he did, right?" someone said.

I grew alarmed. "No. What did he do?"

"He fucked his teenage daughter's best friend."

"Oh," I said.

It turned out that Tom from Tallahassee had gone where even Lester Burnham hadn't dared to go. When his transgression was discovered, Tom had lost his wife, his job, his daughter, his family, and his house. He also presumably had to register as a sex offender. I don't know what else happened to him legally, but it was enough that he'd chosen to flee the U.S. and hide out in Medellín.

This is a book about taking risk—but that was an idiotic risk to take. Nobody should do that.

The hookers in Medellín are called *prepagos*, or "prepaids", and they're legal. I had a reason to hire them too, given what I was going through with the collapse of my marriage. I like to think God would've understood if I had. But I never went to them. Transactional sex is gross, and the truth was I didn't want to give money to any woman for anything at all. I'd suffered a massive rejection, and mostly I needed to know that women wanted me *for me*. The universe won't ever reward me with a cookie for my restraint, but so be it.

———

THE BIGGEST RISKS I took in Medellín were going on a lot of different dates. But I met the women in public, in good neighborhoods, and didn't do stupid things. Today, the scopolamine druggings have grown so common in that city that I would never take the same risks. Back then, in 2014, the criminal gangs hadn't yet infested the foreign dating market.

My Spanish improved quickly. There is no stronger motivation to learn a foreign language than meeting a beautiful lady over a glass of sangria who does not speak English. You have a chance to impress her, if you can just express yourself well enough, or make the right kind of local joke. It's totally on you.

One of those dates didn't go anywhere at all romantically, but it became an important relationship in my life. Her name was Erika, and once we'd shaken hands, she said that she didn't want to date me because I talked about soccer too much. I disputed that, but she was firm in her rejection. Instead, she suggested that we begin meeting for free Spanish lessons over dinner, once or twice a week. She worked in the *alcaldía* (mayor's office) doing community outreach and wanted to establish good relationships with the foreign visitors who had been transforming the city of Medellín.

I eagerly agreed. I needed friends too.

Erika introduced me to hundreds of details of life in Colombia, and I took a lot of notes. I'm amazed at how patient she was with my terrible conversation skills. At first, I would get a headache after thirty minutes of fumbling conversation. Over time, my verbal stamina gradually increased, and I could speak in mediocre Spanish for a couple hours. On my last week in Medellín, we went away for a weekend to a beautiful mountain town in Antioquia—just two friends, sharing a hotel room. That was fine by me. I was grateful to have a friend in a foreign country.

We've met up many times in the years since—in Cartagena, in Bogotá, in Chicago. My new wife was skeptical of our relationship at first, but now she adores the Colombian too, and looks forward to seeing her. Erika is the queen of loyalty.

Originally, during my sabbatical, I'd planned to snake down the western side of South America, tracing a southern route along the Andes, through Ecuador, Peru, and Chile. Soon I realized that would be too ambitious, too difficult, and too expensive. Plus my bag was heavy. This was all before remote work became feasible, so I wasn't earning any money either.

Instead, I chose to stay in Colombia, spending another six weeks in Bogotá, Santa Marta, and Cartagena. From there, I took a weeklong backpackers' boat cruise to the San Blas Islands and onwards to Panama City. I arrived home in

Michigan three days before Christmas and slept like the dead.

It was a big risk traveling to South America alone with modest language skills. But it made me a better, tougher person. It reinvigorated me at the worst time in my life. It taught me a whole new way of life. It gave me new friends, a new worldview, new joy, and a new way of being. And it leveled up my spoken Spanish to intermediate.

Five years later, I would take another risk and pursue the same life—but on an even grander scale, with a much longer timeline. That would change my life even more.

17

A SECOND CHANCE IN THE SECOND CITY

Picture it: a freezing Sunday afternoon in Wicker Park, one of the most gentrified neighborhoods in Chicago.

It was the middle of January, and the worst weather of the winter had already arrived. Over six inches of snow had been dumped on the ground the night before. The wind howled like the screams of the damned.

Inside the warm coffeehouse, I watched cold dark creatures trudging past the windows, shoulders hunched against the arctic whiteness. I'd been one of those creatures an hour earlier, when I'd made my own way through the blurry whiteout in the strange neighborhood.

I was there to meet a date.

My cappuccino sat steaming in its chunky mug on the cheap low coffee table. I wore a heavy sweater, jeans, and winter boots. I was sitting on the edge of a small love seat, talking animatedly and gesturing with my hands.

But I wasn't speaking English. I was speaking Spanish.

In the United States.

I'd officially become divorced just three weeks earlier, and I'd arrived in Chicago two days earlier to claim the keys to my beautiful renovated third-floor apartment in Uptown. It featured a fireplace, a sunroom, two bedrooms, two-and-a-half bathrooms, two balconies, and modern finishings.

I was living there alone, except for a cat that I'd inherited during my divorce. But I felt like I'd won the lottery. I'd returned finally to the Midwest, where I belonged. I had a gorgeous new home, at least by my standards. I was going to take my careers in writing and education in new directions.

Here, at this coffeehouse, sitting in the chair next to me, was a beautiful forty-year-old woman with brown hair, luminous Mediterranean eyes, and a mouth filled with enormous white teeth. Her name was Lucia, and she was a native of Barcelona. She was in the U.S. on a work visa, living and laboring as a director of financial analysis for the Chicago wing of a Spanish firm.

I yammered on and on in her native language. It wasn't unwelcome: she actually seemed to encourage it. Later, she told me that she was checking to see if I was like all the other white American guys who claim to be able to speak Spanish but whose range of knowledge only extends to *yo quiero una cerveza*.

I fortunately had a lot more than that. During one of my pauses, she said, "You speak Spanish like a Colombian."

"Yes, that makes sense," I replied.

"But it's not correct Spanish," she said.

I looked at her face for signs of trickery. Her eyes danced with something I couldn't quite describe.

"But I speak correctly in Colombia," I said.

"Maybe," Lucia replied, "but it's the wrong Spanish."

Her eyes were inscrutable. I couldn't really tell if she was joking or serious. I'd been to Spain once, seven years earlier. I'd heard about Spaniards showing European arrogance towards Latinos.

"Is there a *correct* Spanish?" I said.

"Yes—mine."

She said it with no trace of joking. I sipped my cappuccino. "So I'm guessing you won't ever call me *papi*." That was a South American term.

"*Ay por Dios no*," she spat, feigning disgust. "But don't worry. I'll teach you the correct way."

She and I stayed together for the next five years.

Lucia took my intermediate Spanish and elevated it far beyond what I thought possible. She made me totally fluent. I achieved it through daily conversation, blunt repetition, and a boatload of new bilingual friends.

Her Chicago social group was composed of a couple dozen other Spaniards and Latinos. Soon I was being invited every weekend to multiple different social events, where I held my gin-and-tonic tightly while listening to the lightning-fast Spanish banter ricocheting around the group. I went to FC Barcelona watch parties. On the lakefront, I played volleyball with visiting professors from Madrid and Bilbao. I discovered that the Spaniards are always out socializing, no matter where they are in the world. They are great gatherers, and they never forget any of their friends. It's their greatest superpower.

As a result, my listening skills went through the roof. My speaking skills followed on its heels, and as one of very few Americans in their group, they sometimes needed me too. I became part of the crowd. In fact, Lucia and I hosted the group's annual Christmas party, which always went until four-thirty am.

For our first three years together, Lucia and I mostly communicated in Spanish, with bits of English thrown in.

"*Cariño, como estas,*" I'd say when she came home.

"*Agotado, tio,*" she'd respond. "*Eso puto analista no hace su puto trabajo.* I think I'm going to have to fire her." She loved to swear. The Spanish make a regular habit of it. *Hostia no me jodas* is a common one. They also use *tio* (uncle) the way we use *guy* or *dude*.

"*Que pena,*" I'd say.

Weeks stretched into months, and months stretched into years. We traveled together—Bolivia, Chile, Nicaragua, the Yucatan peninsula, Iceland. I let Lucia speak in Spanish more often than I did, but I still listened closely. I began catching more jokes, more subtleties, more unusual expressions. I discovered that Bogotá and Madrid were the two easiest dialects for comprehension, and that Chilean Spanish was incomprehensible.

She served as my guide as I entered the highest level of my long battle with Spanish, one that had begun twenty-five years earlier.

Then I reached the final boss stage: I went to Spain to meet Lucia's family. For ten days, I stayed in her mother's house. Her mother lived just outside Barcelona, in a town called Granollers, and she didn't speak a word of English. She didn't speak a word of Catalan either. She was born in southern Andalucía and had moved to Barcelona as a young woman and refused on principle to learn a second language, despite the fact that for fifty years everybody around her had been speaking it.

Her mother was a difficult, cold person, but she was a brilliant cook. I would sit in her kitchen and watch the old woman put together *las croquetas*. I asked her to narrate her movements. Her southern accent was clipped and mumbled but it was helpful to build an ear for that.

The most challenging test was Cristina, Lucia's best childhood friend. With an MBA and a career in Spanish media, she was highly educated, highly verbal, and highly uncaring about whether I could understand her or not. I remember being jetlagged at a tapas bar in Madrid while she peppered me with long stories and superfast sentences. I struggled to respond and sometimes resorted to *Claro, claro* ("of course, of course"). Six hours and an equal number of bars later, I literally fell asleep on my feet, standing up like a horse, a glass of wine in my hand.

Overall, the Castellano (the formal term for Spain's Spanish) version of the language is very well enunciated. That makes it easy to understand—more signal, less noise. But the rate of speech is the problem. Spain has the second-fastest spoken language in the world, just behind Japanese. In fact, they speak an average of nine syllables per second, as revealed in a 2019 study. Watch a morning chat show from Spain, or any television program really, and you'll notice it right away. I dare you to try to speak that fast in English.

Experts in brain health recommend learning a new language in midlife to build new neural pathways, rejuvenate your memory, and prevent cognitive decline. I believe that learning Spanish did all of that for me.

In fact, the benefits of becoming fluent in a second language are still revealing themselves. I became mentally sharper, learning very advanced math to better help high-level educational clients. I clarified a lot of oddities about English syntax and diction, which helped my writing and educational work. Later, my fluency helped me secure a position with a

South American firm that appreciated my deep familiarity with the culture and language of its clients. Finally, Spanish emboldened me to later become a digital nomad, which I never would've tried otherwise. That experience yielded me an incredible new wife and a renewed direction in life.

So even though my relationship with Lucia didn't pan out at the end—you can read about that failure in *Strikethru*, the companion volume to this one—she gave me the gift of language.

18

THE OLDEST GUY ON THE FIELD

A common sign of middle age is the male need to tell people that you're still the athlete you always were. I'm just as susceptible to that boast as anybody else.

Unlike others, however, I proved it.

The only competitive sport I ever really loved to play was soccer. As a child, I spent twelve years at center back, then gave up the sport after high school. A dickhead of a coach had soured me on the game, and I felt frustrated with my own weird adolescent body. The bad taste stayed in my mouth for years afterwards. I'd barely watched the sport at all in my twenties, except for a few World Cup matches.

Now, years later, during my divorce, I dipped my toe in the water again. In truth, I'd been mulling the idea of returning to soccer throughout my thirties, but my weird work schedule had made it impossible to follow through. I also didn't like exerting myself in the southern California heat.

But then life changed, and I made good. During a summer spent in southern New Jersey, I started playing in a weekly pickup game. I surprised myself with how much I still loved the sport. After moving to Chicago, a city packed with adult sports leagues, I took a deep breath and signed up for a men's house league team.

I was forty years old. Most of my teammates were in their mid-twenties.

We played on a pitch in Lincoln Park, across Lakeshore Drive from North Avenue Beach, and sometimes on fields located further north, at Montrose or at Foster. The league issued us schedules, uniforms, referees, full 11 v 11 matches, rules, and even huge floodlights so the games could extend late at night. The matches were 55 minutes long and the turf was made of synthetic grass with crumbly bits of black rubber that reduced impact on joints. My knees and ankles were very thankful.

Taking the field for my first game, I slipped into the role of center back like a hand into an old glove. All my muscle memory and instincts reawakened. After a few weeks, my body readjusted to the running, cutting, blocking, kicking, leaping. I learned to hydrate like mad prior to the matches, to avoid pulled muscles—I was sometimes peeing behind a tree when the opening whistle blew. I also stretched my legs and hamstrings for fifteen minutes before every game, since injuries are more common over age forty.

Soon I'd fallen in love with the sport again. I ended up playing for four and a half years, all year round.

THE LEAGUES WERE COMPETITIVE, due to the thousands of good players living in Chicago. A lot of squads were based on ethnicity. I played against Vietnamese, Croatian, and Jamaican teams.

But the best team in our leagues was made up of recent

graduates of the Purdue University varsity team. I'd put them up against any Division II university squad. My challenge, as center back, was to figure out a strategy to limit the destruction. I ended up marking their center forward, a classic sneaky little cherry picker. He was a fast little assassin, and I kept myself a step or two away from him for the full hour. He hated me, but I loved him. He made me a better defender. We always lost, but I loved the matches.

The most fun occurred when our team would suddenly fuse together. I could feel the invisible click, and as a group we'd suddenly shift into a higher level of play. It didn't happen a lot, but when it did, it was as addictive as meth— but much healthier.

During the winter, the games shifted to indoor 7 v 7 matches at the Chicago Fire Pitch, the official MLS practice facility of the Chicago Fire. They put up a huge bubble dome and hung nets from the ceiling to divide the pitch into four smaller fields. I'd been skeptical of indoor soccer, but I soon learned to love the faster, smaller game. The occasional ten o'clock pm start time on a weeknight made me feel bad for players who had an early wakeup the next morning.

It wasn't all sunshine and lollipops though. One player on my team popped his ACL in front of me. After he limped away, we never heard from him again, and he stopped responding to us. Another time, our own goalkeeper went into a full grand-mal seizure near the end of an indoor game. Fortunately, we had a young surgeon on our team who handled the situation.

Once, an opponent with zero understanding of the laws of physics came running full tilt towards me, screaming. I don't know what kind of strategy he was pursuing. I'd already passed the ball, and he was six inches shorter and fifty pounds lighter than me. Confused, I braced my back leg and held up my forearm.

The point of contact turned out to be his throat. The kid ran straight into it. He dropped dropped to the ground, clutching his neck, making gurgling noises. He'd clotheslined himself.

But nobody had seen what happened. The game stopped: his teammates accused me of punching him in the neck. I explained: *He did it to himself!* The weirdo had evidently decided that the one thing he was missing in his life was a broken larynx. My guess is that he was special needs, but I never found out what happened to him.

Anyways, a few individual players stood out.

- A striker, Nick, the fastest person I'd ever seen in my life. Six feet four and built like a greyhound, he'd been a former all-American sprinter at the University of Notre Dame. It was like having Usain Bolt on your team. He couldn't score to save his life, but he sizzled on the field.
- A chubby unshaven slob who captained a team named after himself. I didn't understand how they could be perched at the top of the sixteen-team league. Then the whistle blew, and I quickly understood. Under his beer belly, the slob was composed of one hundred percent fast-twitch muscle fiber. I've never seen an overweight person run that blazing fast. Frustrated, I started grabbing and tripping him. His team went undefeated that season and he scored an average of three goals per game.

Nature hands out its blessings to the people you least expect.
- A weird hybrid creature with the balding head and wrinkled face of a 55-year-old man but the lithe body of a 25-year-old professional athlete. He moved with the ball like a wizard. I couldn't strip the ball off him—and I can strip the ball off *anybody* at the amateur level, and some higher-level players too. At halftime, huddled with teammates, I even offered five dollars to anybody who could take the ball off him. Nobody could. We found out later that he was a high-level coach, with decades of experience. It showed.

Overall, I discovered that it was easy to find certain types of players in the house leagues. Midfielders were by far the most common. They're the workhorses of a squad. Lots of people can get along on a soccer field playing left or right mid. There's no real pressure, they don't play near either goal, they just run and keep things flowing. In fact, I played on one team that was literally fifteen midfielders and me. Goalkeepers are not exactly plentiful, but not impossible to find either. I even filled in that wretched position at times.

The rarest amateur player of all is a good striker. There aren't too many finishers playing for fun in the adult leagues. Those guys usually get picked up for club, college, and professional teams early on, so they almost never go back and play lower-level ball. It was a constant frustration.

I never injured myself, but I did fall hard and suffer some huge bruises on my thighs. Most often, I experienced heavy DOMS (Delayed Onset Muscle Soreness) two to three days after each match, especially strenuous ones. I used to arrange my work schedule around the anticipated soreness, working in my home office on Thursdays. This was mandatory, as a man in his forties playing against well-conditioned men in their twenties.

The good news was that I played much better than I had as a teenager: better positioning, better passing, better leadership. My running speed was good too, given my age—I only met a small handful of strikers who could beat me on a breakaway. The one real handicap I noticed was in my stamina. As a teenager, I had about 65 good minutes in me. In middle age, that had now shrunk to 45 minutes, sometimes less.

I tried a few new moves. When possible, I experimented with fake turns, double pivots, heel flicks, misdirection through hand gestures, arms thrust out to ward off strikers. I learned to return keepers' sky-high punts using my head at the half-line. My friend Hugo, a soccer coach affiliated with the FC Barcelona organization, sometimes joined my team. He later connected me with a couple of higher-level teams, and I filled in for them at center back without embarrassing myself.

Remember, during this period, I was anywhere from ten to twenty years older than the other players on the field. I was beating back the ides of middle age with the broom of boldness.

During those years, I played nearly 150 matches. Leaping off the cliff into the first game every season always felt like a huge physical and emotional risk. I always felt nervous. *What if I play badly? What if they see I'm old?* I never did, and if they knew my age, they never said anything.

Playing soccer changed me for the better. My body felt

younger, my heart and lungs grew stronger, my sleep deepened, my passion for life increased. During a decade in my life when most men are watching televised sports with beers in hand, growing depressed, I was playing *hard*, once or even twice a week, and feeling energized. In fact, if I ever become health dictator of the world, the first thing I'll announce is that for every one hour a person spends *watching* a sport, he or she must spend one hour *playing* that same sport.

Unfortunately, I was forced to stop playing in March of 2020, when the pandemic interrupted everything and shut down all public activities. And then my life drastically changed again, for many years.

19
YES IS MY DEFAULT SETTING

During the last decade, my nonfiction writing career has consisted mostly of ghostwritten books and educational materials. In that time, I've learned how to win writing assignments.

I always give the same answer.

Yes.

If they ask you, "Can you—" or "Do you know anything about—" or "Would you feel comfortable—"

The answer is always yes.

It doesn't matter if that's the truth. I was a ghostwriter for four years in Chicago, and when my firm asked me if I knew about a particular topic, they always received the same answer.

So, do you know anything about chicken farms? Oh, yes —I love learning about cutting-edge poultry rendering techniques. (A complete lie.)

Hey, we have an assignment about toxic workplaces. Are you familiar with that topic? Absolutely! I've worked in so many bad office environments. (Not true.)

Do you think you can write a 25,000-word handbook on dementia next week? Of course, send the assignment along! (I knew nothing about any neurodegenerative disease.)

ANOTHER COMPANY once asked me if I'd be interested in updating their AP Human Geography title, which sold tens of thousands of copies annually. They already trusted me from my updates of other titles over the previous years, including European history.

Did I know anything about human geography? No, but I said yes anyways.

Here's my reasoning: if they were asking, they *wanted* me to say yes. I just gave them the answer they were hoping for. I knew that I could learn the material quickly: human geography was adjacent to everything I already knew well (history, languages, social studies).

I bought a couple of textbooks, a couple of prep books, read up on the topic, watched some videos. Then I dove in and updated their title. The company was pleased, and I did the same updates for several years afterwards. I eventually wrote all the exams for that course.

Later, I leveraged that experience to become a lead SME (subject matter expert) in the field for two other educational companies. I've led teams responsible for building state curricula from Georgia to Oregon. And I've had 80 or 90 private tutoring clients as well, from Silicon Valley to Swiss boarding schools.

All because I said yes.

I understand that "fake it til you make it" isn't applicable to many situations. A microbiologist applying for a grant wouldn't be able to wing his research in quite the same way. But it's possible in certain fields, especially if you know your own ability to learn on the fly.

I know what you might be thinking, and no, this isn't unethical. If we all took assignments that we only had previous experience in, nobody would grow or develop. We'd be stuck in a societal loop of decay. There has to be some play in the wheel. The next generation has to squeak into positions of responsibility, even if they're not always fully qualified. On-the-job training is real.

If you compare it with the strict vs. loose interpretation of the Constitution, I'm on the side of the Federalists. Our powers don't always have to be explicit. They're implied.

―――

In fiction, I've taken risks too.

In the field of independent publishing, a podcaster and brand-merchant named Rebecca Syme has identified four types of author archetypes. This schematic can be applied to any creative industry.

The four archetypes:

1. Trailblazer—This artist needs to be new, original, and different.
2. Drafter—This artist follows the trailblazer, reads trends, pivots quickly, and becomes the person others follow for advice.
3. Evergreen—This artist follows the drafter, avoids risk, and writes squarely to market.
4. Island—This artist doesn't listen to advice, doesn't care about business, and writes what he

wants. The work can be either original or written to market.

I'm a mix of several, but in my choice of topics I've usually been a Trailblazer. I don't want to write yet another iteration of the same old police procedural that you've read or viewed a hundred times. I always need to find a new angle on an old story.

For instance, I've had trouble categorizing my Ainsley Walker Gemstone Travel Mystery series because it doesn't fall easily into a known subgenre. It's a light mystery, yes, but it features tropes from cozy books, action-adventure, and women's fiction. Somehow the series has been moderately popular.

Likewise, I'm currently preparing a trilogy of YA books from the public domain. These titles were well-known when they were published in 1900, but today they're crying out for a huge edit. So I'm redoing some of the plots, characters, descriptions, and pacing. I'm claiming the derivative works as a new copyright and putting my author name on the covers next to the original author's name. I don't know of any other publisher doing something like this; most YA is original. I have no idea if these stories will be successful. They could very well flop. But the challenge fascinates me, and the books will stand out in the market.

Trailblazer, see?

This is not to bash people who are Drafters or Evergreens. In fact, I have purposely tried to find ideas for the future that are less original and written closely to market. But so far I've taken risks by writing things that don't closely follow anything else.

During my ghostwriting period, I was called upon to take creative risks and write a wide variety of stories.

International aviation thrillers. Cartoonish stories about spirit puppets living in an abandoned mine. Lesbian BDSM murder mysteries. Science-fiction astral projection stories based on esoteric philosophy.

I tackled all these projects with no fear. That's why I kept getting hired. It feels like surfing. The more waves you catch, the less fear you have about catching another one.

20
IN THE LAND OF SAND AND MINARETS

In 2019, I was recommended for a job on an unusual team of college admissions counselors.

At that point, I'd been working part-time in private college admissions counseling for sixteen years. I enjoyed the work, but it never seemed like something to pursue more intensely. Guiding undergrad and graduate applicants through the sometimes-byzantine application process is a seasonal occupation, like snowplowing, something you do from September to January. But there's a big foreign market for this type of work, since international applicants are often in the dark about the process.

This company was different. The principal partner, Bob Stanley, a former corporate litigator with an Ivy League background, had a contract with a major educational foundation in Saudi Arabia. The mission: to help the best and brightest of that country's high school students achieve admission into the best universities in the Western world. Bob's team had been assigned 200 students—and later, 400—for nine months of extracurricular activities counseling. That would be followed by five months of weekly application help. He needed one more person to round out his team.

During my interview, one of the first questions out of my mouth was, "So who runs this foundation?"

Bob took a deep breath. "That's a good question. It's founded by MBS."

I didn't know much about Saudi Arabia, but I knew that name. MBS was Mohammed bin Salman, the young future ruler, the crown prince of Saudi Arabia. He was the one assassinating his domestic enemies on foreign soil. In fact, he was the one behind the Jamal Khashoggi murder—and Khashoggi had been associated with *The Washington Post*, my former employer.

Those are *terrible* things.

But at the same time, MBS was transforming the repressive, backwards-looking Saudi culture of petroleum extraction and forced Islamic piety into a forward-looking society of the future built on renewable energy. He and his cohort have envisioned a network of highly advanced cities along the Red Sea built upon sustainable energy and the integration of digital technology with everyday life. Look up the city of Neom.

Those are *wonderful* things.

As someone once said about another Prince, the musician—MBS is either a bad guy with a lot of good days, or a good guy with a lot of bad days. It's hard to tell.

"I would be helping the girls too?" I said, thinking of all the women forced to wear *hijabs*.

"Oh yeah," said Bob. "More than half the students are female."

After we ended the call, I grappled with the morality of this position. Saudi Arabia is like the sleazy, wealthy friend of the United States. He sells us the black liquid we need, and he pretends to like us for transactional reasons. Deep down, though, we know this guy hangs out with awful characters, and talks about us behind our backs.

I came to this conclusion: Taking this job would mean taking money from one of the most misogynistic cultures in the world. But I would be doing so to help its brightest young women escape to the West for education. I could help expose them to Western norms for a few years. I would play the Robin Hood of civil liberties.

I saw this as a slight win. I accepted the position.

The work itself wasn't risky. Through new video conferencing tools like Skype and Zoom, I chatted with Arabic teens halfway around the world. The girls often wore hoodies to cover their hair, even online.

Then, a few months after I began, the Saudi foundation invited our team to come to Riyadh for the orientation ceremony for next year's students. They would pay for the airfare and the hotel.

That was a risk.

Most of the females on the team declined the offer, but I and three others accepted it. With some exceptions—Russia, China—international travel is a risk I'm always willing to take.

ONE SHORT FLIGHT to Riyadh later, however, and things changed.

It was a strange week in Saudi Arabia. I'd prepared some Arabic phrases, but I didn't need too many of them. The city is packed with foreigners, since Saudi imports guest workers from India, Bangladesh, and elsewhere. Most of those service workers speak English. This means that you can order food at cafes and takeout places in English, just the same as anywhere else. Hotel workers typically speak English. I even saw some Pakistani cricket games in the city.

Overall, the climate in Riyadh felt strict and rigid. That's because of Wahhabism, the repressive branch of Islamic philosophy that has controlled the Saudi state for the last half century. Wahhabi beliefs led to the *mutawa*, the infamous Saudi religious police. Its deputies used to chase people out of shopping malls at prayer time, hand out fines for dress code infractions, and scream at members of the opposite sex who dared intermingle.

But MBS took apart that goon squad in 2018. He defunded the religious police. Many Westerners don't know this.

Clothing was a question mark. I didn't quite know what to expect regarding women's dress. Here's what I found. Among Saudi women, about three-quarters wore the simple *abaya*—a long black robe—together with a head covering. That was the default. Some women wore it tightly, others wore it loosely, revealing normal clothing underneath. The loose style was a new development.

The other quarter of the women, however, wore the full *niqab*, which is a head-to-toe black drape. It covers every part of the woman's body, including the face, except for a single cutout for the eyes. The *niqab* has a long tradition on the Arabian peninsula: it's centuries older than the Saudi state, which was founded in the 1940s. I imagine the practice was developed to cope with the brutal heat of the Arabian desert. Contrary to Western belief, wearing a *niqab* isn't mandatory. Mostly, it's a sign that you come from an extremely conservative family, and only a minority of women wear them.

A few of my teenage clients had already met me online

wearing the *niqab*. That was a weird experience: I was basically talking to a black curtain with eyes on my screen. In person, one of them came up to me, saying my name: I had no idea who she was. There were no identifying characteristics, which is the point.

I also found that the females wearing the *niqab* were almost always more rigid in their thinking than the other female students. I attribute that to the type of mindset that one builds after a strict lifetime of following the strictest religious codes on the planet. The females in the *niqab* usually planned to study engineering or computer science, which was no surprise: the most inflexible thinkers are drawn towards engineering. It can be a noble field—it literally builds civilization—but the work is allergic to ambiguity of any type. This is why extremists feel comfortable in the field. More than a few scholars have noticed that radicalized terrorists tend to have engineering backgrounds, including the Saudi ones responsible for the September 11 attacks.

In Riyadh, I visited the Diplomatic Compound, a huge neighborhood filled with foreigners and the Saudis connected with them. I went to three different high-end shopping malls, with their pristine, glossy floors. Wealthy middle-aged Muslim women draped head-to-toe in black strolled in pairs, carrying Prada and Gucci bags. Exploring the city on foot, I headed towards the Jarir bookstore, a popular chain, and was surprised to find the top floor filled with English test-prep and language books—including a couple I'd contributed to. The English section was equal in size to the Arabic section.

One night, my team went out to eat at a Lebanese restaurant where I surprised our waiter by ordering *kibbeh nayeh* (raw lamb ground with couscous), using its Arabic name. I'd grown up eating it at my Lebanese babysitter's house. Lebanese cuisine is kind of like the Italian food of the Middle East; everyone loves it, everywhere. Across the region, you can always find a plate of hummus, *taboulleh*, and *baba ganoush*.

I noticed a lot of construction on storefronts. It was curious. An American living in Saudi Arabia explained to me that, under Wahhabism, all public facilities used to have mandatory double entrances: one for men, the other for families (meaning women and children). But MBS had lifted that restriction only two weeks before I'd arrived. Now storeowners across the country were rushing to modernize to a single entrance at last.

Saudi Arabia had modernized its immigration services too. Until 2018, the Saudi tourist visas used to be difficult to obtain: I'd heard that you had to go for an interview at an embassy or consulate, and the process took at least a month. Today, you fill out a simple form on a website. I received my visa by email in ten minutes. Likewise, the suspicious Wahhabis used to require most Western visitors to be accompanied by a minder for their entire stay. MBS has removed that restriction too, and I wandered through the capital on my own, unmolested.

During a VIP tour of the city, I was taken into a clothing store to be fitted and fussed over for ten minutes. I found myself draped in Saudi menswear—the famous *thawb* (white robe) and red-and-white checked *keffiyeh* (headdress). Then I found myself thrust out on the sidewalk, totally draped in traditional Saudi garb. I walked around the city like that for the rest of the night. It wasn't unpleasant. Passing Saudi men nodded at me in approval. If my headpiece slipped a little, a stranger would come over and adjust it for me.

Overall, the city of Riyadh was safer than most places

I'd lived in the United States. I've thought about returning to Saudi Arabia someday, mostly to visit Jeddah, the ancient port city on the Red Sea known for its slightly looser way of life and its exciting film festivals. But I've also read horror stories about the regime holding U.S. travelers hostage if it's decided that their online presence, or real-life activities, stand in opposition to MBS' goals. That type of risk doesn't sit well with me, so my experience on the Saudi peninsula is probably a one-and-done. You have to know where to draw the line.

Leaving the country, I spent another ten days in Dubai.

That metropolis, one of two major cities in the UAE (United Arab Emirates), is a massive consumer oasis. Springing up out of the desert in the last fifty years, Dubai is where the Middle East goes shopping. It's a forest of brand-new black curtain-wall skyscrapers, all labelled with the names of the same few construction firms. Shopping malls and plazas are what passes for civic culture there, and the pedestrian sidewalks are filled with hundreds of different types of humans. I was surprised to hear very little Arabic spoken. English is the lingua franca of the world, and I got around with no problem.

Then I spent a day crossing the desert in a rented black Mercedes to visit Abu Dhabi.

That's a hell of a city. It's the old money counterpart to Dubai's new-money flash. In Abu Dhabi, the Louvre has opened a stunning contemporary desert-inspired structure. Likewise, New York University has built a beautiful satellite campus there. Most spectacular of all was the Great Mosque of Abu Dhabi, a brand-new masterpiece. Most mosques prohibit non-Muslims from visiting, but this one encourages it. Be sure to go a few hours before sunset—and remember to behave conservatively. The guards will confiscate your camera and delete photos if you're acting even the tiniest bit inappropriate. That includes making any kind of hand gesture in a photo, even a peace sign. They booted out the pop star Rihanna a few years ago for an inappropriate photo shoot, even though she was dressed totally in black.

Finally it came time to leave the Middle East. This was the first week of March 2020. I'd been hearing news reports about a new virus that had been popping up in places around the world. Then it hit: the day before I was scheduled to leave, Abu Dhabi closed its airport to prevent further contagion. I grew nervous and doublechecked my flight out of Dubai. It was still scheduled to go.

I did in fact squeak out, but my 14-hour flight back to Chicago was less than a third full. I slept fully stretched out in my row with the armrests lifted. The pandemic descended upon the world completely. A few days later, the UAE ended all flights, other less fortunate travelers were marooned inside the country for several months.

As for the Saudis, I worked with them for the next four years, until our team finally lost the contract. We might win it back—never say never—but right now it looks like my experience with the Arabian peninsula has reached its end.

21
MY JOB FIT INTO MY BACKPACK

While I was gone to the Middle East, my then-girlfriend Lucia had decided to purchase a new condo, on her own, without me. This should give you a sense of the weak state of our relationship.

Nonetheless, she invited me to give up my apartment and accompany her to her new place. That was a sign of sunnier skies ahead, and after five years inside the same four walls, I was ready for a change anyways. I rolled the dice, trusting in her usually good judgment.

Most importantly, I downsized, selling more than half of my furniture on Facebook Marketplace. The stuff was over a decade old and stank of long-past divorce: I was happy to lose it. In retrospect, doing this was an excellent decision. I had also sold my decade-old Ford Escape the year before, another equally fortunate decision.

By May of 2020, I found myself living in a Tribeca-style open-floor-plan loft in the Lincoln Park neighborhood of Chicago. We were still in the first stage of the pandemic, and Lucia and I were living and working together in a single large room. In other words, we were on top of each other, talking all day to our laptops, with no end in sight. She began resenting me as an obstacle to her efficiency. I took a temporary office nearby, but it didn't move the needle on our relationship.

Her attitude towards me deteriorated fast, and I didn't have the will to fight for us. In July, I finally ended the relationship. There was some obligatory yelling, but she found a pebble of self-awareness and accepted the inevitable. For the next few nights, I lay there on the couch, thinking about my next move.

It was a weird time. The epidemiologists said that another wave of covid-19 was on its way that winter, and it would likely be worse due to the cold weather. A vaccine was nine months away at minimum, they said. The winter holidays would undoubtedly be cancelled. I would very shortly be homeless, and I'd already sold two-thirds of my furniture. If I wanted to reestablish myself in Chicago, I'd be in for a long, cold, lonely winter in a mostly empty apartment.

Then my mind turned to politics. I'd watched the BLM marches plunge straight down Halsted Street that summer, thousands of people spontaneously assembling via Twitter. Thoughts of 1968 danced through my mind, and I worried about what was else was coming down the pike that winter, given the 2020 presidential election. After all, we'd elected The Joker to national office, a psychopathic con artist in orange clown makeup. I was worried that he might stir up the populace in a never-before-seen way, and that things might get violent. (The half-assed coup attempt at the Capitol on January 6 didn't surprise me at all. I'd assumed it would be worse and more widespread.)

In short, between breakups, disease, politics, and civil

unrest, life in the U.S. wasn't looking too attractive. It would be a good time to get out for a while.

Next, I looked at my work. Outside of my writing, the pandemic had helped me pick up many new clients and companies in my educational career. Prior to the virus, half of my work had been online. Six months later, it had all gone online, and more was being added every week. I was doing quite well.

Then I took stock of my personal life. There were a lot of things I didn't have, for better or for worse, things that other people my age had willingly pursued. I owned no home, always preferring to rent for the flexibility. I no longer owned a car. I no longer had a girlfriend or a wife. I had no children, to the best of my knowledge. I had no need to take care of my parents, who were elderly but independent. My extended family and friends didn't depend on me for anything either, except for messages and emails and phone calls and funny stories. As a freelancer, I didn't have coworkers; I couldn't be recalled to an office at the end of the quarantine. I had some credit card debt, but the balances were low.

In short, there wasn't a lot tying me down anywhere.

Then I took stock of the things I did have. I was enjoying a rapidly growing income. The pandemic was arbitrarily lifting certain sectors of the economy while destroying others, and I'd been one of the lucky ones. I knew that my employers and clients didn't give two drips of runny shit where I lay my head at night. I was free to go anywhere I wanted, as long as there was a dependable wifi connection.

Then there was the medical consideration. I've always enjoyed excellent health, part from luck and part from habit. This mattered a lot in a virus-driven pandemic that took delight in killing people with comorbidities. The official IFR (Infection Fatality Rate) for my age cohort was about 1-in-450. That of course was massively overestimated, since it only counted documented cases of covid-19, and we know that millions of people recovered alone, at home, without any official record of their illness. The real denominator in that ratio was likely quadruple the official estimate, so the chances of me needing medical care anywhere in the world was very small.

(That said, if I'd been obese, or immunocompromised, or afflicted with metabolic syndrome, I never would've left the US. I would've absolutely stayed close to home and top-notch medical facilities.)

Plus, as noted, I had already built fluency in Spanish. Most of all, I harbored a strong desire to explore the world. It's a big place, and we should go see it all. Check out my other books, if you don't believe me.

In short, I was free to leave—if I wanted.

I had set up a series of dominoes in my life, some on purpose, some by accident. Now the universe had added a few more: a MacBook Air, a global pandemic, the spread of broadband, and a new videoconference application called Zoom. All of this made a remote working life possible. All of these things made the concept of an international digital nomad life possible. People were already doing it. I'd read about them in the past, from the safety of my couch.

I could be one of those people. All I needed to do was touch the first domino. But first I needed to admit to myself that I *wanted* to do this.

I breathed out, looked at the ceiling, and made my final decision.

Yes.

I would become a digital nomad.

Leaving the US in September of 2020 felt like one of the biggest risks I'd ever taken. Certainly, getting out of the country was an ordeal. It was a time when very few were traveling. The world was girding its loins for the anticipated second wave of the pandemic.

Trying to arrive in Barbados, my first stop, was a comedy of errors. First came a month of cancelled flights by American Airlines, then a cancelled connecting flight in Dallas, then an involuntary ten-day stay in Miami Beach (expensive but not unwelcome), followed by a rebooking on LIAT airlines. (LIAT, I found out later, colloquially stands for Late, If At All.) That flight, however, required a forced five-day stay in Jamaica, in quarantine, while waiting for a new connecting flight to Barbados.

It was my only option, and once I arrived in Kingston, I was greeted with the task of finding a new PCR test (as my last one had expired) in a developing Caribbean country, on a specific day (Wednesday), at a specific time (three o'clock pm), to qualify for the 72-hr PCR rule that Barbados had in place for arrivals. Achieving this was a feat that required the help of the PR guy at my hotel, who placed a personal call to the actual Jamaican Minister of Health (a childhood friend, he explained), whose office obtained me a single spot at one of two private clinics on the island. The private clinic only took cash, which had to be paid on the morning of the exam. The hoops were leapt through, and I was tagged onto the butt end of a large group of people. Jamaican authorities also placed a mandatory app on my phone to monitor my whereabouts, though it's not clear that anyone ever followed up on that. I left the phone in my hotel to go out for dinner twice. Color me rebellious, but I hadn't been to that island since age five and wanted to see what I was missing.

Finally arriving in Barbados, I sat in another mandatory eight-day quarantine. A man draped in a full hazmat suit brought carb-heavy foods (pasta, club sandwiches, fries) to my hotel room door three times a day. I felt like the Christmas goose being fattened before the kill. Leaving the room wasn't allowed, either, even though I could hear the ocean crashing just thirty tantalizing meters away.

Later, after being released, I discovered that while Barbados had zero cases of covid, they still enforced all the new global protocols. So I spent the next three months wearing masks everywhere, getting temperature checks in the forehead, and accepting squirts of gel — you know, the same old drill, but *on an island with no virus whatsoever*. They're not particularly good at independent thinking, those Bajans. (This observation has been echoed by others too.) If I sound frustrated, it's because I'd gone there precisely to escape the virus, not to pretend it still existed. Still, Barbados is a tropical paradise, an island of both rural poverty and bourgeois comfort. It's also one of the most successful independent nations in the region, a task that is not easy to accomplish.

Next stop was Colombia. Landing there in January was fairly easy. That country requires a simple 96-hour PCR test, which was easily gained in Miami, and the movement around that terrific country was mostly unrestricted, though there were occasional surprise weekend lockdowns in Medellín that were barely enforced. I'd been to Colombia before, for several months in 2014 and again in 2019, and the people are the most friendly of any place I've ever been.

I avoided Bogotá until the end of my two-month stay there, since the covid-19 situation was so precarious through January and part of February. In fact, if the world ever suffers a pandemic like this again, my advice is to head to warm cities such as Medellin in the months following the winter holidays (January and February). The post-holiday viral bulge there was less pronounced, thanks to the "eternal spring" climate that allows so much outdoor dining, outdoor activities, and outdoor socializing. Bogotá suffered a much larger increase in post-holiday cases simply because of the colder climate there, and the subsequently greater numbers of indoor parties and socializing during the holidays.

In rural areas such as El Eje Cafetero, the open-air coffee region where I stayed for two weeks, locals told me that there was no virus there until November 2020, months after it'd gripped most of the world, and very little transmission of the virus once it arrived. My hired driver said there'd been a total of two covid deaths, both people over age 70. There really is something to be said for fresh air and ventilation in avoiding viruses (see the end of this article). I would guess that better overall health, owing to a life of agricultural labor, probably played a role too.

In March, it was onto Peru, for which I gained another PCR exam in Bogotá, this one administered by a sadistic nurse who jammed her swab into my nose with enough strength to crack a rock. I also discovered that Peru required face shields on all transportation—plane, train, bus, and auto. That was my biggest difficulty.

See, it drove me a little batty to wear both a N95 and a face shield, because together they create a sonic bubble around your skull in which you can hear both your own breathing and your own words bouncing back at you. Then imagine going to a check-in desk at the airport and trying understand a Latin female with a small, high-pitched voice speaking to you rapidly in a foreign language

—while she wears two layers of facial protection and stands behind a plexiglass shield. I'm fluent in Spanish, but I don't have superhuman hearing. Instead of asking people to repeat themselves, or inflict another excruciating hand-cupped-to-ear conversation, I would sometimes just say yes, and then hope that I'd hadn't just agreed to a five-year term of indentured servitude. This was sometimes true in restaurants too, even excellent ones such as Maido. Please go: the tasting menu was probably the best meal of my life.

Overall, Peru was very strict about covid-19. At Machu Picchu, for example, there were spotters standing throughout the historic mountaintop site who were ready to reprimand anybody who took off the mask for even a second. It didn't matter that the site was as open air as a place can possibly be.

Still, that famous wonder of the world, as astounding as it is, was overshadowed by a day tour of the Sacred Valley I'd done a few days prior. My overall favorite site in Peru was definitely La Reserva Nacional Salinas y Aguada Blanca, outside of Arequipa. The high point of the year (literally) was bathing in natural hot springs at 15,000 feet (5000 m) elevation in the middle of a hailstorm next to a mini-volcano while watching llamas wander by.

Mexico was more relaxed. I'm not sure if that's good or bad. There was no PCR exam required for entry, and I'd estimate that only about 75% of the people on the street in Mexico City were wearing masks (compared with almost 100% everywhere else). Sometimes I'm not sure the older people understood that they were in the midst of a pandemic. I saw hundreds of maskless older folks gathering in large groups in plazas for salsa or ranchero dancing. So keep that in mind next time you want to curse out Americans. We haven't cornered the market on intransigence, but we definitely complain the loudest.

After that, I received the free J & J vaccine at Miami airport, and so ended a very unusual chapter of not only world history but also personal history.

WAS TRAVELING DURING A PANDEMIC DANGEROUS?

No more than staying at home in the US. After all, you can socially distance anywhere, in any country. In fact, I'd argue that a warm climate, good ventilation, outdoor activities, personal fitness, social distancing, and the almighty N95 mask are all you need to avoid any serious viral illness. Where you do these things matters very little. The only exceptions are those who are immunocompromised, elderly, or afflicted with metabolic syndrome (obesity, diabetes, high blood pressure, etc), in which case it's best to keep oneself in the most developed country possible in case of hospitalization. For those of us in great health, I have yet to see any dangers in traveling during this pandemic.

Did people think I was crazy?

Yes—fear is much stronger than hope. Friends and even my own family told me to stay in the US during the pandemic. This would've meant an entire Great Lakes winter sealed alone behind closed doors, which seemed like a silly thing to do when I saw a second, even bigger wave of infections coming.

Plus, when the world says zig, I like to zag. I see this flexibility as a positive attribute during times of crisis—it's the old principle of throwing yourself into the punch instead of waiting to be greeted by it. I cast aside fear and made judicious decisions regarding risk. That meant looking at the miniscule IFR (infection fatality rate) for people my age, a number that included the obese and metabolically afflicted. Plus there was my own suspicion that I had already had a mild five-day case of covid-19 in January 2020, months before it became A Thing.

As a result, I safely explored four new countries, visited bucket-list sites for half price, gained tons of new story ideas, made a lot of money working online, met a ton of new people, and fell in love with my new wife. I never would've met her if I hadn't traveled abroad.

Would I do it again?

Yes, absolutely. Choosing to travel internationally during a global pandemic was one of the best choices of my life. *Crisis* is the Greek word for "turning point" or "decision"—something all good storytellers should know—and I benefitted from this one in a thousand ways.

22
LOVE IN THE TIME OF LOCKDOWNS

Confession: I shaved six years off my age on my dating profile. It was a tiny risk that has paid off infinitely well.

Here's what happened.

When I found myself thrust back into the dating pool, I didn't have much appetite for the game. I'd spent too much time dating—fourteen years of my adult life, to be exact—and I'd been turning up zeroes for too long. The phrase *unlucky in love* pinged around my skull a lot. I knew I wasn't alone in this. There are many pots who never find their lids, and it occurred to me that I might stay a lonely pot forever. You can read more about this in *Strikethru*, the companion memoir to this one.

Still, I wearily decided to open accounts on Tinder and Bumble, the two most popular dating apps. I like meeting people in person whenever possible, but during a global pandemic, there wasn't much of that happening. The in-person dating market, what was left of it, had retreated totally onto the phones.

I came to the screen to enter my age. I paused and thought for a moment. I was 44 years old and happy with it.

I liked my appearance, my experience, my talents, most of my choices. But at some point in my thirties, my aging process had slowed to a crawl, and I began looking a lot younger than other people my birth age. I'd found that mentioning my age could trigger people's worst feelings about themselves, so I took care to avoid the topic.

My pet theory is that everyone has an ideal age that they belong at. Mine is 35 years old, so I figured I would find a thirtysomething woman to date. I've always gotten along well with people in their thirties. In fact, when I was 25, I preferred dating women in their thirties: younger women annoyed me with their immaturity.

But there was a problem. Thirtysomething women are petrified of turning 40, especially if they're single. Therefore, on the apps, many of them will set their "seeking" age to a maximum of 40. To date a man over that age would mean admitting that they themselves aren't spring chickens anymore. And many women would sooner die than admit that.

Of course, none of this matters in person. In the flesh, a man has a thousand different tools to create attraction, and age doesn't really factor in. But the pandemic didn't afford in-person mixing. We were all on the apps, where age range unfortunately is mandatory.

So, swallowing my distaste, I listed my age as 38. It was a lie designed to gain more online visibility to women in their mid-thirties, my ideal age. I figured I would explain the lie to anyone who cared enough to meet me.

After arriving in Barbados, I was sitting in my quarantine hotel room on a hard mattress. I had little to do for nine days but sit and read, sit and write, sit and feel my butt growing flatter with inactivity. So I opened Tinder.

To my surprise, I ran out of facecards quickly. There were only about 25 women on the entire island on that app. I wasn't too disappointed. I hadn't come to the island to date. I'd come to avoid the pandemic, work online, read some ebooks, maybe write a book, do some long-distance swimming, post up at a rum bar.

I matched with a few women. One was a 42-year-old mother of seven children whose estranged husband had a drug problem. Not my type. But she nicely brought a bag of coffee to my hotel and had it sent up to my room during quarantine. That's Bajan hospitality. She was a good one.

A second match was a sketchy woman from Toronto who claimed to be a sommelier. I went out with her but quickly pegged her as a not-too-bright schemer. She ditched me near the end of the date to go hang out with her male "friend" who she'd previously described as really, really, ridiculously good-looking. I was happy to see her leave.

My third match was a 26-year-old named Ashley. That was young for me, but I liked her photos: she looked sweet and very pretty. Her bio was suspiciously short. She said that she loved Netflix, cookies, and dogs. Nothing more.

A couple weeks later, Ashley and I met. She was fresh out of a bad marriage and wasn't looking for much of anything. Strolling the ocean boardwalk at night in the tropical breezes, we found that we both had master's degrees in English. We both were writers. We both digested stories the way other people digest sandwiches. We both worked in education. We both loved seafood. We both valued kindness in others.

And she was beautiful. Really beautiful.

I hadn't been looking, but she seemed perfect for me. I hoped the feeling was mutual.

It was. We soon became inseparable. Literally, we were together 23 hours a day; she only peeled herself away to go feed her dogs. I worked six days a week while she lay on my bed writing her first novel. We planned field trips on Fridays; she drove me to see different parts of the island, such as Soup Bowls on the east coast and the Wild Animal Reserve in the north.

Still, I grew worried. I only had three months in Barbados. I couldn't stay, but I didn't want to lose her either.

So I took another risk. After only a few weeks of dating, I invited her to travel the world with me. Ashley immediately swatted down the offer. She couldn't do that. She had a job. She had four dogs. She didn't know me like that.

I shrugged. Shooting for the moon isn't supposed to work.

A week later, though, she quit her teaching job. She now claims that it was bound to happen anyways, that she'd been unhappy there for a while. That's debatable. I found out later that she'd also been inquiring if her parents would be willing to take care of her dogs for an extended period of time.

A month later, Ashley let me know that she had begun to consider my offer of travel. By the end of my three months, she'd tentatively accepted. We agreed that she would pay for her own airfare, but I'd pay for the apartments, the food, and the entertainment.

I met her parents for dinner one night, so we could get to know one another. I liked them immediately, which boded well for the future. We had a lot in common. For their part, they were mostly checking to see that I wasn't a sex trafficker.

Let's cut this long story short. Ashley and I spent the next two years traveling the world together—South America, Canada, the U.K., Europe. Then I proposed to her, we were married, and now we're life partners in every possible way.

Writing the story now, it seems like a dream, a covid-19 love story. I stumbled into the ideal woman at the ideal time. We smoothly fell in love and began what gives every indication of being a lifelong partnership.

But finding Ashley was the culmination of a series of risks, big and small. I took a risk to sell my car and many of my possessions. I took a risk to end a dying relationship with Lucia. I took a risk to become a digital nomad. I took a risk to travel internationally during a pandemic. I took a risk to get to Barbados when the airlines kept canceling the flights. I took a risk to shave six years off my age on a dating app, which was the only way she could've matched with me (her upper age limit was set to exactly 39). I took a risk to meet a strange woman in a foreign country.

All these small choices led to a place where very few people go, especially at a time when nobody was choosing to go anywhere. And she was waiting for me there, like a golden chalice at the top of a long flight of stairs.

23

A NOTE ABOUT THE FUTURE

I'm too young to have written this book, but I wrote it anyways.

My life is going strong, and many more risks still await me. Ashley and I have begun a small publishing company together, and we've splashed into all the emotional compromises that a marriage requires. If we're lucky, a baby might be on the way someday, which would be a whole new type of risk. I've got many wild business plans in mind, plus a few more on the athletic field, but there's no point explaining those before I've tried them.

I hope that some of my life experiences have been instructive. To older readers, they've maybe served as a mirror to reflect upon your own choices in life. To younger readers, they've maybe inspired you to step outside the lines and take some of your own risks.

Educated young people in the West have mostly swallowed the same messages for their entire lives. Always remain cautious, always color inside the lines, always act when instructed to do so.

But that isn't what makes a rewarding life. That isn't

what creates entrepreneurs. That isn't what creates intellectually curious adults. That isn't even what makes a good civilization.

This needs to change.

I'm optimistic. I'm confident that we'll swing the child-raising pendulum back towards a healthy expression of assertiveness. In the meantime, those of you born in the late nineties and the oughts will have to learn that taking risks means embracing ambiguous outcomes.

Jump off that cliff and build your wings on the way down.

PLOTWORKS PUBLISHING

If you enjoyed this book, please leave a review wherever you purchased it.

Then visit Plotworks Publishing to check out J.A. Jernay's companion memoir, *Strikethru*.

Turn the page for a sneak peek—

J.A. JERNAY
STRIKE THRU
a memoir

my history of failed relationships

FROM THE AUTHOR OF THE AINSLEY WALKER GEMSTONE TRAVEL MYSTERY SERIES

CATALINA

Southern California is packed with barely functional head cases. *Tip the world over on its side*, said architect Frank Lloyd Wright, *and everything loose will land in Los Angeles*. It makes dating there a real chore. Everybody's got a relationship horror story.

Age twenty-six is when guys start to get cuffed by baby-minded women feeling the pressure of too many lost uterine linings. It's the age when many of us begin to turn our eyes towards mortgages, promotions, a full night's sleep. It's the age when a large number of eligible men find themselves yanked off the dating market and cajoled down the wedding aisle.

But none of that happened to me at age twenty-six.

Instead, I met Catalina.

She worked at the office where I read scripts. Catalina had short black hair and big brown eyes and a large toothy smile. She also had a photogenic face, a bit like Marilyn Monroe.

Like that famous woman, Catalina suffered from

borderline personality disorder. But I didn't know that right away.

I started messaging her on a primitive messaging service —AOL, I think. I flirted and cajoled and begged her to come out with me. At some point, she caved in, and we embarked on a crazy summer.

My roommate at the time, Noah, was skeptical. He was exactly the type of best-friend character in a movie who cocks his head and asks the protagonist: *Are you sure you know what you're doing?*

Of course I did. (Narrator voice: He didn't.)

* * *

At age thirty-one, Catalina was five years older than me, and her behavior was extreme. She'd been through a weird string of huge professional ambitions, followed by quick collapse of those same ambitions. At one time, she'd fully decided to become a film director, until about a month later, when it dawned on her that she'd never be as big as Steven Spielberg. So she immediately gave up. She'd once impulsively shaved her head totally bald. Another time, I watched her leap off a roof into a swimming pool, that famous party stunt you see in movies that can go so horribly wrong.

Mostly, she was directionless.

It turned out that she was seeing a therapist who'd recommended to her that she not date anybody, because she wasn't emotionally stable enough. The therapist had urged her to start baking as a way of grounding herself during episodes of dissociation.

Catalina started ridiculous fights with me, fights that wouldn't end until I removed myself from her presence. Most of those spats began on the flimsiest of offenses, or on straw men, or on figments of her imagination, or on nothing at all. Once, at a social event on the Sunset Strip, I was chatting with a female attorney when Catalina grabbed me and pulled me out to the sidewalk and yelled at me for my enormous insensitivity. Then she began convulsing at the waist: she was suffering a panic attack, triggered by the sight of me speaking to another woman. She pulled a tab of Xanax from her purse and swallowed it. I drove her home and put her to bed.

At other times, she'd suddenly decide to break up, claiming that she didn't want to become a Midwestern housewife. I don't know where that claim originated from. At the time, I didn't want to return to the Midwest, and I didn't want that from her. But the made-up version of me that existed only inside her crazy skull evidently was making a lot of racket. I shouldn't have taken her seriously, but I did anyways, charging forward with my spear of logic into her viper's nest of irrationality. It did no good whatsoever. She was just like a maze, as John Mayer sang, all the walls continually changing.

After the breakups, Catalina would change her mind again, and come over to my apartment with a tray of cupcakes as an apology. I'd bite my tongue to stop from pointing out that baking cupcakes is a very Midwestern housewife thing to do.

My roommate Noah loved the apology cupcakes. "She's crazy," he said, wiping his mouth with a napkin, "but she knows how to bake."

PLOTWORKS PUBLISHING

Turn the page for a sneak peek of *The Oxford Diaries* by J.A. Jernay!

THE OXFORD DIARIES
A STUDENT TRAVELOGUE

J.A. JERNAY

SEPTEMBER 10

This afternoon, with the energy of a cartoon-hyper, sugared-up toddler, I stepped onto a punt at Magdalen Bridge. Instead of using that wonderous invention called the paddle, Oxonians have instead opted to retain their reputation for efficiency in all pursuits and furnish their boaters with poles. This makes it impossible to push in a straight line. Punts bounce from bank to bank like air hockey disks.

To make a prickly situation even worse, I was pulling the punt from the front—a Cambridge tradition—rather than pushing from the rear in a more Oxford fashion. Such faux pas. Alexandra also did my back a great favor by steering me into a nest of picker bushes.

That night we dined on value meals at KFC with Gerda, then met a Paki friend named Shariq who had a couple bottles of cheap Bulgarian wine, added them to our two bottles of cheap stuff, and traipsed down to the Thames. A full moon, a scenic riverbank, four people, four bottles of alcohol. Nothing but lapping water and happy gulping and tinkling laughter.

Then, in a burst of surrealism, a longboat suddenly cut through the night. It was a party boat sailing down the river, directly before our eyes, from right to left. It carried three hundred brightly-lit partygoers, the drunkest ones hanging off the sides of the boat and whooping like monkeys. "Dancing Queen" by Abba was coming across the water.

Behind the party boat were four teenage boys rowing a skiff in its wake, trying desperately not to lose the party. They saw us, gave up, and paddled over. Docking on the riverbank, they climbed up on the lawn and entertained us for an hour. One taught me the local tradition of punching knuckles together and saying, "Respect!" Another claimed that his older brother's band had just been offered an opening slot for Pearl Jam. Skeptical, I asked for the name, and he said Supergrass. I'd never heard of them. A third told me that my cricket jacket (wool sweater) marks me as a tourist. A fourth one claimed that he wasn't racist because he went to Ireland once.

Finally the boys hopped into the meadow behind us and gamboled about in the bright moonlight like pubescent centaurs.

PLOTWORKS PUBLISHING

Visit Plotworks Publishing today for all these titles—and more!

ABOUT THE AUTHOR

J.A. Jernay is the author of nearly 80 different works of fiction and nonfiction. He is married to fantasy author A.J. Renwick. He lives in Michigan.

www.ingramcontent.com/pod-product-compliance
Lightning Source LLC
LaVergne TN
LVHW091300080426
835510LV00007B/337